D1013607

WHY SO MANY GODS?

TIM BAKER AND KATE ETUE

NELSON REFERENCE AND ELECTRONIC PUBLISHING

NASHVILLE

A DIVISION OF THOMAS NELSON. INC.

WWW.THOMASNELSON.COM

WWW.XT4J.COM

Published in Nashville, Tennessee, by Thomas Nelson, Inc.

Extreme for Jesus™ Brand Manager: Hayley Morgan
Extreme for Jesus™ Acquisitions Editor: Kate Etue

Page Design: Matt Lehman, Nashville, Tennessee
Cover Design: Pointsize Associates, Glasgow, Scotland

Library of Congress Cataloging-in-Publication Data

Baker, Tim, 1965-
Why so many gods? / Tim Baker.
p. cm.
ISBN 0-7852-4763-7
1. Christianity and other religions. 2. Religions. I. Title.

BR127 .B27 2002
261.2—dc21

2001044939

Printed in the United States of America
02 03 04 05 06 PHX 5 4 3 2 1

TABLE OF CONTENTS

TABLE OF CONTENTS

WHY RELIGION MATTERS

Everybody has some kind of religion. "What?" you say. "I don't believe in God—I don't have religion." Well, your lack of religion is like your religion. Everyone needs something to believe in. They need something bigger than themselves to be a part of (even if it's the belief in nothing). Our whole life is a search for identity; we're trying to figure out who we are and why we're here. People have come up with lots of different opinions on the matter over the history of mankind, but they're all trying to figure out how this place called earth works.

In this book we're going to take the position that Christianity is the only true religion. That it's the only one that makes sense. Why? It's the only one where God actually saves His creation. In all the other religions in this book man saves himself. What's the big deal with that, you ask? Well, if man can save himself, why does he need God?

If Christianity is true, and we'll show you later how to know it is, then it's pretty darn important. 'Cause if it's true, and you're ignoring it, then you'll have hell for eternity. Really. This guy a long time ago named Pascal thought up something that's now known as Pascal's Wager. He said that if God exists, he'd better believe in Him. If he doesn't, he's in trouble. If He doesn't exist, then it doesn't hurt him to believe in Him while he's alive, so he might as well believe. Get it?

HOW TO DECIDE

As we said in the "Why Religion Matters" section, Christianity is the only religion where God is really God, because it's the only one where God saves the people instead of the people saving themselves. But how do you go about proving to someone that God even exists in the first place? Well, these are some of the tried and true arguments for the existence of God.

1. DESIGN. If you were walking around in the forest and stumbled on a Rolex, would you think to yourself, "Wow! It's amazing how this watch just formed itself from nothing out here in the middle of nature!" No. You would say, "Cool. Some rich guy lost his watch and now it's mine." But really, you would assume it was purchased at a store that got it from a warehouse where some guy works on an assembly line making them all day long. What's the point, you ask? Things with intricate design point to a creator. The universe is pretty intricately designed, who made it? God. (The Big Bang, etc. doesn't hold up here. If a printing press exploded do you really think Webster's Dictionary would just form from all the letters they've got sitting around in there?)

2. ONTOLOGICAL. This one's kinda heavy, so follow me here. **God, by definition, is perfect.** Or, God, in order to be God, must be perfect. In order to be perfect, **He has to be perfect at everything.** That means He has to be perfect at existence. So, in order for God to be God, He has to exist. God can't have started the world then disappeared or anything like that. Because God is perfection, He must exist.

3. COSMOLOGICAL. This one's deep too. Okay, everything that happens has to have had a cause. Your car moves because you started the engine. The engine started because the key turned. The key turned because . . . and on and on. The world and our existence have to have a cause. There has to be a final cause—one thing that started everything—for it to all make sense. In order for it to be final, it has to be perfect. That cause has to be perfect. Voila! God.

4. ENTROPY. You learn in high school the second law of thermodynamics. The amount of energy in something is decreasing—we're moving from a state of order into a state of chaos. That means that at the very beginning, there must have been a state of order. (This also disproves evolution—we aren't moving from disorder to order.) So, way back when, there must have been perfect order. Chaos now, perfect order at the very beginning. Once again, the only answer is God.

Christianity
WHEN GOD BECAME MAN

SHORT HISTORY

Christianity goes back to the beginning of time, so its history is really, really long. But we'll start about two thousand years ago—when Christianity became different from Judaism. That was because of Jesus. You know the Christmas carols—silent night, shepherds, wise men, angels. The cool thing is that it's all true.

Jesus was born in a manger (what animals ate out of) and grew up in the area that's Israel now. The Bible doesn't tell us about His teens and twenties, but when He was about thirty He began what lots of pastors call His "public ministry." He started preaching and performing miracles all over the Palestinian area. He had twelve disciples—guys who lived and worked with Him and believed that He was God. Then, three years later, He was crucified. The religious leaders did this because they thought He was a heretic when He said He was God's Son. But, three days later, He rose from the dead—making good on all His promises and the prophecies of the Old Testament.

The Christian church has had lots of twists and turns since then. Its history hasn't been spotless (think: the Inquisition, the Crusades, yada yada), and it has a ton of branches—Catholic, Orthodox, Baptist, Presbyterian, Charismatic, Anglican, Episcopal, Methodist . . . the list goes on. But for the past two thousand years it's been a pretty huge force in society, and it's the largest religion on the face of the earth.

BASIC BELIEFS

Christianity is the only religion where we don't have to work our way to God. He left heaven to come to earth to save His people—we don't have to do anything except believe Him. Jesus is the Son of God. He was born to a virgin girl named Mary—the fact that she was pregnant was a miracle, a God thing. Everything in the Holy Bible is true.

Christians believe that people are sinful from the get go and need a savior. Thank Adam and Eve. When God created them, they were perfect, but they chose to eat the fruit they weren't supposed to and that's where we got sin. Read about animal sacrifice in Jewish law—it was the way God set up forgiveness in the Old Testament. But then Jesus came to earth. Why? Because we couldn't do it on our own. We needed a sacrifice that was pure and without blemish, to take on all our sins like no goat could. We needed a perfect sacrifice—enter Jesus.

Jesus comes in to save the world, not with an iron fist but with an invitation. An invitation to get up close and personal with the God of the universe. He offers the only way to get to Him. Jesus Himself became that way. Accept Jesus, accept God. Deny Jesus, deny God. No more priests, no more third-person-removed. Through this guy, Jesus, we all have access to God.

Jesus had to die as the final sacrifice for all sin—past, present, and future. But the kicker is that He rose again after that horrible death, to sit up in heaven with God, because God cannot die, and Jesus is God made man.

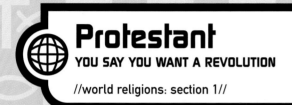

Protestant
YOU SAY YOU WANT A REVOLUTION

//world religions: section 1//

SHORT HISTORY

The protestant church has its roots in the whole protestant Reformation. Here's an easy way to look at it. Before the mid to late 1400s A.D., the Catholic church was the key church in the western world. Everyone who went to church went to a Catholic church. The people believed in God because they always had, and because believing in God explained the way the universe worked. Hardly anyone outside the leadership of the church ever read the Bible (heck, they really didn't even have a Bible they could understand because it was all written in ancient languages). Then a dude named Martin Luther came along.

Martin Luther was a poor guy. His dad saved all his money so Luther could go to school. He went to school in Germany (because he was German), and was supposed to go to law school (his dad wanted him to go), but Luther was almost struck by lightning one day, and decided that it was a sign for him to become a monk. He entered a monastery (where monks live) and became fascinated with God's Word. He hated that the Bible was locked away where the common person couldn't get to it.

At the same time, Luther noticed a movement in the church called the Indulgence movement. This was where people could buy salvation for their dead family members. The church made loads of money off of this, but it really couldn't do what it promised, which upset Luther. He also didn't like the fact that the church claimed to be able to forgive people; the church had removed God from the act of forgiveness.

Luther was all about the Word of God. It was his measuring stick for everything. So, when he noticed the whole indulgence thing, and the fact that regular ordinary people couldn't read God's Word, he began to act. In opposition Luther nailed a document called the 95 Theses to the door of a church. **The Ninety-Five Theses listed ninety-five reasons why it was wrong for the church to sell indulgences.** From there, Luther was in all kinds of trouble. He was excommunicated and threatened a lot. But once he stood against the status quo, Luther began a movement that became bigger than he was. It started people thinking about a new way to look at God. It put God's Word in the hands of the common person.

BASIC BELIEFS

GOD EXISTS: This is a basic belief among protestants. Protestants believe that God eternally exists, and we can have a relationship with Him through Jesus. Protestants believe that we can know God and know about Him through reading the Bible, thinking about Him (using our rational minds), and learning about Him from other people (like pastors, Sunday school teachers, etc.). In the Bible, He is called our Heavenly Father.

JESUS: He is God's eternal Son. He was present at the creation of the universe and throughout history, He walked the earth, He was crucified for our sins (so we can have a relationship with God), and He rose again and lives in heaven. Jesus is often called The Word made flesh.

THE HOLY SPIRIT: God's eternal Spirit sent to earth to teach, inspire, convict, and guide. You read a lot about the Holy Spirit in the book of Acts (especially in the first few chapters). He's often associated with power and miraculous events—even in our day.

SCRIPTURE: Protestants look at God's Word like it's directly from God's mouth. They read 2 Timothy 3:16 (check it out) as proof that the Bible they use is from God. Protestants believe that God's Word is without error.

GOOD VS EVIL: Protestants talk a lot about the evil that's in the world. They attach the idea of evil to Satan, an angel who lived in heaven with God until he decided to do things his own way. They admit that there's evil in the world—and God allows the evil to exist for a short time for a reason.

SACRAMENTS: Protestants believe that Jesus began two very important sacraments—the Lord's Supper (a.k.a. Communion) and baptism. What are these sacraments, and what makes them so important? Well, they're the two "ritualistic-type" things that Jesus actually participated in on earth (in other words, Jesus was baptized, and He started the Lord's Supper when He had the Last Supper with His disciples). Jesus made it clear that He expected believers to keep doing these two things after He went to heaven.

FAITH: Protestants use their minds to think about God, and they use their reason to decide whether He exists or not. But, many believe that there comes a point when reason does not work. In other words, you can't think your way to God. You've got to have faith. Faith is a trusting obedience in the work of Jesus who died instead of you to pay the penalty for your sin. Your faith makes God happy.

FOLLOWERS ARE CALLED:
Christians, Protestants

HOW DO YOU BECOME A CHRISTIAN?

You have faith in Jesus Christ that He is the Lord of your life and say that with your mouth. It's as simple as that. No initiation, no physical torture, no hours of research or meditation. "By grace you are saved through faith" (Ephesians 2:8). That means we don't deserve it, but if we believe, we'll be saved anyway.

WHAT'S THE ATTRACTION?

It's permanent. Once God saves you, you don't have to do any "work" to keep Him loving you. He is the perfect Father you never had. You know from that day on you are eternally loved. He promises to never leave you and never forsake you. And best of all, you have the creator of the universe on your side.

WHAT'S THE GOAL?

Relationship and union with God through faith in Jesus.

GOD:	The Trinity—God the Father, God the Son, and God the Holy Spirit. Three in one.
FIGUREHEAD:	Billy Graham is one of the most famous Christian pastors around, but protestants don't have one person in charge of all of them.
AFTERLIFE:	Heaven or hell
WORLDVIEW:	Monotheistic
SACRED TEXT:	The Bible
WORSHIP SERVICES:	In churches, usually on Sunday morning
RITUALS / RITES / SACRAMENTS:	Protestants take Communion, and they get baptized. The amount of ritual varies a ton between the different groups, though.
DID YOU KNOW?	82% of American teens claim to be Christians.
GEOGRAPHIC CENTER:	The religion started in the Holy Land, Israel, but now it has spread to almost every country in the world.
NUMBER OF FOLLOWERS:	2 billion worldwide 224 million in the USA

SCENE 1

EXAMPLE OF BELIEFS IN POP CULTURE:

"The real battle's just begun
To claim the victory Jesus won
On Sunday, bloody Sunday
Sunday, bloody Sunday."

U2, "Sunday, Bloody Sunday"

"Nobody in U2 understands where this music comes from . . . I have to believe that [God] is where it comes from . . ."
—Larry Mullen, Jr., drummer for U2

CELEBRITIES:

Bono, rock star
Jessica Simpson, pop musician
Lauryn Hill, musician
Lance Bass, member of *NSYNC

THE TRICK?

There's no trick here. Christianity is unique because it's the only religion where the believers can't save themselves. Their God is actually God because the people are completely lost without Him.

Catholicism
HAIL, MARY

SHORT HISTORY

This branch of Christianity goes back a long way. How far back? To the time Peter and Jesus are standing up on a mountain. Jesus says, "Peter, I'm going to build my church on you buddy. Here's the keys . . . let's get to work." (okay, this is a paraphrase. Want the real words? Check out Matthew 16:19) And from there, the first sermon preached by a disciple was by Peter (check out Acts 2). People came to know the Lord, and the church was born.

From this point, a lot of Catholic beliefs are about Peter and his authority. Peter was the first pope, and he ruled and organized the first church. When he died, the authority of the pope was passed on to another man (a guy named Linus), and then to another guy, and then another. In all there were four other popes in the Catholic church before the end of the first century A.D. This formed something called an "Apostolic Succession." While the pope today isn't Peter himself, he's like Peter, because he's a direct descendant (via "Apostolic Succession") of Peter.

Since the very beginning, the Catholic church has been highly accepted and has remained part of the fabric of many cultures. It's hugely influential in the lives of its members. Often, people will say "I'm Catholic" before they'll say, "I'm Christian." Kinda shows you the force that the Catholic church is in the world today.

BASIC BELIEFS

CATHOLICS BELIEVE THE BASIC CHRISTIAN THINGS—LIKE JESUS WAS GOD'S SON AND HE WAS GOD. HE CAME TO SAVE US FROM OUR SINS.

• GOD AND JESUS AND THE HOLY SPIRIT: Catholics believe in the same God, Son, and Holy Spirit that other Christian churches do.

THE NEXT THREE BELIEFS ARE FOUND ONLY IN THE CATHOLIC CHURCH, NOT PROTESTANT:

• SAINTS: Catholics pray to God, but they also request that Saints pray for them too. Sometimes people see the way they revere saints and think that Catholics actually worship the saints. That's not true. But, they believe that Saints are in the presence of God and pray for people on earth.

• MARY: Jesus' mom gets a place of reverence and devotion. She's just a little lower than Jesus and just a little higher than the saints.

• IMMACULATE CONCEPTION: It's the belief that Jesus' mom was sinless at her conception (because Jesus couldn't be born from a sinful woman).

FOLLOWERS ARE CALLED:
Christians, Catholics

HOW DO YOU BECOME CATHOLIC?

You convert. It's a lot like becoming a member in any church. There are membership classes to attend and all that.

WHAT'S THE ATTRACTION?

Being a part of the family church. Forgiveness of sins. Connecting with a priest (an earthly representative of God). Reverent worship services.

WHAT'S THE GOAL?

Forgiveness of sins. Spending eternity in heaven with God. Getting to know great saints in the church.

GOD:	The God of the Bible
FIGUREHEAD:	The pope
AFTERLIFE:	Heaven for some people. If a person needs to be cleansed before going to heaven, they go to Purgatory where they make up for their sins. Anyone who dies without hearing about Christ or being baptized are left to the mercy of God.
WORLDVIEW:	Monotheistic
SACRED TEXT:	The Bible, New American Version
WORSHIP SERVICES:	In a church or cathedral. There are different styles of worship services. Some services are formal and might seem reverent. Other Catholic services use more contemporary worship music.
RITUALS / RITES / SACRAMENTS:	There are seven sacraments in the Catholic Church. **BAPTISM:** Catholics baptize infants before they experience a spiritual conversion. Infants are welcomed into the church community through baptism.

RITUALS / RITES / SACRAMENTS (CONT'D):

CONFIRMATION: Once a person has been baptized, they go through confirmation as an adult. The purpose is to offer the adult believer a chance to make a personal choice for the Christian faith. The Bishop prays that the person will receive the Holy Ghost, then makes the sign of the cross on their foreheads with Chrism (a mixture of olive oil and balsam) and asks that the peace of God be with them. Then, the person is blessed.

HOLY EUCHARIST, OR COMMUNION: The Eucharist has distinct effects in the life of the Catholic. It signifies union with Christ. When we take the Eucharist, we're becoming a part of Christ and the church—there's both a spiritual and mystical union that happens.

PENANCE: After confessing your sins to a priest, you are told to do a penance (like "pray ten Hail Marys," etc.). This is how you are forgiven of your sins.

THE SACRAMENT OF ANOINTING THE SICK: This is the sacrament in the Catholic church that used to be called Extreme Unction. It's dedicating a sick or dying person to God. Catholics do it, but they're not the only ones—MANY Christians do this.

HOLY ORDERS: This is when someone dedicates their life to the ministry of the church as a deacon, priest, or bishop.

MATRIMONY: Marriage. Two baptized people becoming partners for life.

DID YOU KNOW?	If you see the word *catholic* with all lower-case letters, it means *universal*.
GEOGRAPHIC CENTER:	The Vatican City in Italy. It's actually its own country within the city of Rome, Italy. It's where the pope lives.
NUMBER OF FOLLOWERS:	1 billion worldwide 62 million in the USA

IMPORTANT VOCABULARY:

ROSARY: it's a string of beads that Catholics use when they pray. Each bead reminds Catholics to say a different kind of prayer. What prayers? The Lord's Prayer (Catholics call this the "Our Father"). The Hail Mary (see below).

HAIL MARY: **not the football pass,** it's a prayer to Mary. It goes,"Hail, Mary, full of grace, the Lord is with thee. Blessed art thou amongst women and blessed is the fruit of thy womb, Jesus. Holy Mary, mother of God, pray for us sinners, now and at the hour of our death. Amen."

EXAMPLES OF BELIEFS IN POP CULTURE:

Keeping the Faith was a movie about a priest and a rabbi who were best friends. It shows them in church a lot, so you can see what their worship services are like. Another movie, *Dogma*, is a total slap in the face for the Catholic church. It stars Ben Affleck, Matt Damon, Chris Rock, and Selma Hayek.

CELEBRITIES:

Christy Turlington, supermodel
Mother Teresa, nun

THE TRICK:

No trick here folks. Looking to become a part of a faith that's tied to WAY back? Interested in a distinct church structure? Like the Pope? Then Catholicism might be for you. What's really attractive here? The history. When you're listening to the priest, you're listening to a guy who holds an "office" that's traceable back to Christ.

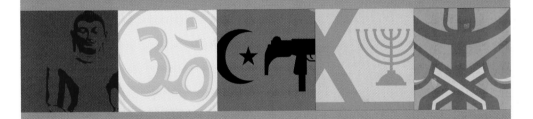

NON-CHRISTIAN WORLD RELIGIONS

Webster's Dictionary says that a religion is "a personal set or institutionalized system of religious attitudes, beliefs, or practices." Huh? Basically, you believe something specific about God or gods or goddesses. You act according to those beliefs. We'll see later how cults and the occult are a little bit different from this.

Bahá'í
VISUALIZE WORLD PEACE

//world religions: section 1//

SHORT HISTORY

You know how Christians believe in the Second Coming of Christ? Well, way back Muslims were waiting for "the Báb" to return. And in 1844, a guy in Iran announced that he was it. His name was 'Alí-Muhammed, but he took the title of "the Báb," which means "door" in Arabic. He said that god sent him to prepare mankind for a "new age" and that another Messenger would come after him and be even greater. Well, thousands of people bought it and followed him, but the government didn't like his gig. Six years later they had him executed.

So, after the Báb died, this other guy, Bahá'u'lláh, said he was that next Messenger that the Báb had talked about. But he wasn't really too popular either, and they sent him into exile in the Holy Land. He wrote a lot while he was there. Bahá'ís use his books as scripture now. After he died, his son and grandson became the leaders of the faith.

Bahá'ís believe god is breaking down barriers between races, classes, religions, and nations. Bahá'ís work hard to get rid of prejudices because they want all people to be treated as part of a big "global family." Bahá'u'lláh wrote, "The Earth is but one country, and mankind its citizens." Kinda makes your heart warm, doesn't it?

BASIC BELIEFS

The main teaching of this religion is unity—one religion and one humanity. Bahá'ís also believe that god is beyond our ability to understand. That's why he sends us Messengers—they teach us and lead us. Moses, Zoroaster, Krishna, Buddah, Bahá'u'lláh—they're all here to teach us about the same god and the same religion. More prophets will be born to give us new messages from god that will change religion. The way Bahá'ís grow spiritually is to listen to god's messengers, pray, and trust god.

Bahá'ís believe there are two sides to religion— spiritual and social. They believe that the basic spiritual teachings—love your neighbor, etc.—are found in all religions. The social side, how the spiritual is acted out, changes according to the time period you live in.

WHAT THEY THINK (Today anyway. It'll change in the future):

- There should be *one* world government.
- You shouldn't be prejudiced.
- Women are fully equal to men.
- The extremes between poverty and wealth should be eliminated.
- Each person can independently search for truth.
- Everyone should be educated.
- Religion is in harmony with logic and science.
- World peace is possible. So is one international language.

FOLLOWERS ARE CALLED:
Bahá'ís

15

HOW DOES A BAHÁ'Í BECOME A BAHÁ'Í

First they investigate the teachings of Bahá'u'lláh for themselves. If they accept that Bahá'u'lláh is god's messenger, then they try to live by his teachings.

WHAT'S THE ATTRACTION?

People dig the idea that we're all **one big family**—women and minorities especially. They also like the idea that all religions come from the same source and have the same purpose—helping humanity progress.

WHAT'S THE GOAL?

World peace

HOW DOES IT LOOK LIKE CHRISTIANITY?

They believe in one god. They believe in Moses and other "messengers of god."

HOW IS IT DIFFERENT FROM CHRISTIANITY?

While they're cool with Christianity, they're also cool with Islam, Buddhism, and any other religion. The Jesus of Christianity says, "I am *the* way, *the* truth, and *the* life. No one can come to the Father except by me." Bahá'ís would disagree with this—they think you get to god through the teachings of Bahá'u'lláh.

GOD:	There is one god, the creator of everything.
FIGUREHEAD:	Nope. There ain't just one.
AFTERLIFE:	After you die your soul continues to get closer to god. Heaven and hell aren't actual places—they're spiritual "conditions." Heaven is close to god, and hell is further away from god. You can experience heaven and hell while you're still alive.
WORLDVIEW:	Monotheistic
SACRED TEXTS:	The books written by Bahá'u'lláh—there are over 100. Here's a quote from one: "The essential purpose of the religion of God is to establish unity among mankind."
WORSHIP SERVICES:	In a temple, no weekly service.
RITUALS / RITES / SACRAMENTS:	They don't have any official priests or clergy, but they've got ceremonies for when you get married or die. Groups get together every nineteen days for devotions, counseling, and fellowship. They fast from March 2nd to the 20th every year. And they are supposed to make at least one trip to the Holy Land to see Bahá'u'lláh's grave.
DID YOU KNOW?	They're in more countries than any other religion in the world except Christianity.
GEOGRAPHIC CENTER:	India
NUMBER OF FOLLOWERS:	5 million worldwide 130,000 in the USA

EXAMPLE OF BELIEFS IN POP CULTURE:

SCENE 1

Have you ever seen those "Visualize Whirled Peas" bumper stickers? Bahá'ís would be totally into that. And in the movie *Clueless* when Cher gives a bunch of her stuff away to the victims of the Pismo Beach disaster—Bahá'ís would support her in that.

★ CELEBRITY: ★

Dizzy Gillespie, the famous jazz musician

THE TRICK:

If the gods from all these different religions are the same god, then why are the messages from all of the prophets contradictory? How do you explain it? You can't.

Buddhism
NO ME. NO DIVINITY.

SHORT HISTORY

It all starts with Buddha, a.k.a. the "enlightened one," who was born about 560 B.C. in India. His mom named him Siddhartha—try living that one down through junior high! He was the son of a rajah, a king. Back then kings had "wise men" around to give them advice about running their kingdom. The wise men here told Siddhartha's dad that Siddhartha would be a "great king" if he followed his dad to the throne. But they also said that if he left home he would become a savior of the world. His dad didn't want a savior; he wanted a king. He wanted his son to "take up the family business," so to say. The king tried to keep him home by spoiling him rotten. Siddhartha got anything he wanted. He lived in luxury and never had to see anything sad or painful.

When Siddhartha hit his twenties, he got married and had a son. He still hadn't left the palace. One day he told his dad, "I want to see the world." Since he got whatever he wanted, his dad said, "Okay." Little did the king know that this trip would change everything, because when Siddhartha was out on those streets he saw old people, poor people, and death. He was puzzled by it all because he had never seen any of it. But then, cha-ching!, it all became clear. Siddhartha decided then and there that he was leaving the palace. He went straight home and told everyone he was going to search for enlightenment. He packed up, said goodbye, and left the palace forever. He was about twenty-nine years old. His followers call this day the Great Renunciation.

So, where was the first place he went to look for enlightenment? **Religion. That would be Hinduism.** As he studied it, he got really bummed out. So he thought he'd try another avenue. Ascetism was his next choice—that's where you totally give up the comforts of life. But that didn't do much for Siddhartha either. So he sat down under a tree to mediate on it.

Now, he's sitting cross-legged under this tree and he finds nirvana, not the band but the highest degree of "god consciousness." Story has it he stayed under that tree for seven days and learned all kinds of truths. He was now the Enlightened One, or Buddha. He was thirty-five years old.

He had been traveling with five monks, so he shared his wisdom with them. His first sermon was the Four Noble Truths and the Eightfold Path. They loved it. So he began to preach his message all over India. The burned-out Hindus loved his message too, and by the time Buddha died, at age eighty, Buddhism was an Indian religion.

With Buddhists now, the historical Buddha (Siddhartha) is not very important. The state of mind of a Buddha is what they care about.

BASIC BELIEFS

FOUR NOBLE TRUTHS

1. All of life is suffering. Birth hurts, death hurts. Getting sick, getting old—it all hurts. Not getting what you want really hurts.

2. Suffering is caused by your cravings and desires. Stuff like wanting to be successful and happy in this life and in your future causes pain.

3. The ending of suffering is possible. Just give up your passions, your cravings, so you have no desires at all.

4. Following the Eightfold Path will end all the pain.

EIGHTFOLD PATH

1. Right understanding of reality. You have to explore and accept the Four Noble Truths and the Eightfold Path with an open mind.

2. Right Thought. You have to renounce all your desires. You can't hate anyone or anything.

3. Right Speech. Don't lie. Don't indulge in idle chatter. No gossip.

4. Right Actions. Don't kill any living creature. Only take what is given to you. And don't commit any bad sexual acts, steal, get drunk, or gamble.

5. Right Occupation. Get a job that won't harm anyone.

6. Right Effort. Be perfect. Do all you can to make sure you have no evil habits or character traits.

7. Right Meditation. Be observant, alert, and free from desire or sadness.

8. Right Concentration. After you've done all that, you have to enter into the four degrees of meditation by concentrating.

WHAT THEY THINK:

- The world evolved.
- There is no god.
- Be loving to all creatures—man and animal.
- Don't give in to worldly entertainment— like movies and TV.
- Don't wear jewelry or dye your hair.
- You can worship idols.
- Don't pray to Buddha—he no longer exists.
- Tithe to the monks.

BELIEFS (CONT'D)

Now, hang on folks. Buddhism breaks into a bunch of different groups.

THEREVADA BUDDHISM: the original Buddhism

MAHAYANA BUDDHISM: popular outside India, mainly in China and Japan

ZEN BUDDHISM: a branch of Buddhism that is big in the U.S. Zen means "meditation" in Japanese

TIBETAN BUDDHISM: the leader is the Dalai Lama

FOLLOWERS ARE CALLED:
Buddhists

HOW DOES A BUDDHIST BECOME A BUDDHIST?

They choose to practice the basic beliefs.

WHAT'S THE ATTRACTION?

Buddhism is very practical, is not dogmatic, and does not require you to give up your religion to practice it.

WHAT'S THE GOAL?

Enlightenment
No more suffering—nirvana

HOW DOES IT LOOK LIKE CHRISTIANITY?

They believe in having good morals. Also, the Eightfold Path looks a lot like the Ten Commandments. They think lying, adultery, etc. are wrong, the same way Christians do.

HOW IS IT DIFFERENT FROM CHRISTIANITY?

The big one: they don't believe in God. They also don't believe in sin, heaven, or hell.

GOD:	None
FIGUREHEAD:	The different branches have different figureheads.
AFTERLIFE:	Reincarnation or nirvana
WORLDVIEW:	Atheistic
SACRED TEXTS:	There's a ton of them, but maybe you've heard of The Sutras? Scriptures are directly transmitted from mind to mind (telepathy) and don't need words to be explained. Zen teachers say, "Look within, you are the Buddha." Disciples have to find their way through self-effort.
WORSHIP SERVICES:	In a temple
RITUALS / RITES / SACRAMENTS:	BURNING INCENSE: an offering to Buddha OUZO: like a rosary, used to count recitations of a mantra A BELL: tells you when your meditation is over MEDITATION: varies according to type of Buddhism KOAN: verbal puzzles that lead you to enlightenment Example: "A cow passes by a window. Its head, horns, and four legs all pass by. Why did its tail not pass by?"
DID YOU KNOW?	The Dalai Lama won a Nobel Peace Prize.
GEOGRAPHIC CENTER:	India
NUMBER OF FOLLOWERS:	300 million worldwide 401,000 in the USA

IMPORTANT VOCABULARY:

NIRVANA: enlightenment. A blissful spiritual condition where the heart gets rid of all passion, hatred, and delusion. It's the highest spiritual plane one can attain, their final goal. No more desire and no more suffering.

DHARMA: law as taught by Buddha. It includes the Four Noble Truths and the Eightfold Path.

KARMA: Do a bad thing, get a bad thing done to you. Do a good thing, get a good thing done to you. It might not happen to you 'till later, but it will happen. Your karma "account" determines your existence now and in the next life.

MANTRA: ritual sound, word, or phrase used to evoke a certain religious effect

EXAMPLE OF BELIEFS IN POP CULTURE:

The Free Tibet Concerts. They were huge in the 90s. Also, the movie *Seven Years in Tibet*, starring hottie Brad Pitt, is a true story about a mountain climber and his friendship with the Dalai Lama.

CELEBRITIES:

Phil Jackson, coach of the LA Lakers
Steven Seagal, actor and martial arts expert
Richard Gere, actor

THE TRICK:

If there's no god, then who brings them back after they're dead?

SHORT HISTORY

The year is 550 B.C. China is at war. The violence is terrible. Some battles have up to 400,000 victims. (To put this in perspective, about 57,000 American soldiers died in the entire Vietnam War.) They killed everybody—men, women, children, and old people. They did horrible things to the victims—like cutting them up and making them into soup. Then they made their relatives eat it. Nasty. Really nasty.

A man named K'ung Fu Tzu—we pronounce his name Confucius in English—lived at that time (along with Socrates, Buddha, and Plato). He hated all this violence and started to speak out about it. He'd go around arguing for human rights, saying all the bloodshed should end. He was huge! Everybody thought he was brilliant. He became world-famous for his wisdom. Mostly, he passed on what he learned from his father and grandfathers—be nice. His report card would have read "works well with others."

The funny thing about Confucius is that he never intended to start a new religion. He just wanted to make the world a better place. But now he's considered a god, and Confucianism is the official philosophy of China.

BASIC BELIEFS

Confucianists believe that there's hope for humans if they would just be nice to each other again. They think our nature is basically good. If we do bad things, it's only because something outside of us made us do them. Knowledge can keep us on the path of doing good, and we learn things by studying the ancients.

They believe that we live in a society influenced by a never-ending process of change. This is called the yin and the yang. Yin and yang stand for the energy forces of good and bad that control our world. As long as we follow the forces of positive change, we're all right. Change is easy; you've just got to look for it. Once you find it, it will take care of itself.

BASIC ETHICS:

Be polite · Love your family · Be righteous.
Be honest · Be kind toward others · Be loyal to the state.

FOLLOWERS ARE CALLED:
Confucianists

HOW DOES A CONFUCIANIST BECOME A CONFUCIANIST?
By following the teachings of Confucius

WHAT'S THE ATTRACTION?
History, wisdom of the ages, harmony with fellow man

WHAT'S THE GOAL?
To help create a peaceful world

HOW DOES IT LOOK LIKE CHRISTIANITY?

It's a very moral religion, so you wouldn't notice anything really "wrong" with it. They promote morality, respect for other people, and peaceful natures. They want people to become better.

HOW IS IT DIFFERENT FROM CHRISTIANITY?

Well, they follow the teaching of Confucius, not God. They don't believe in God, and they think that people are born good. (Christians believe that people are born sinful, which is why we need a savior.) Confucianists also believe that people can change themselves with knowledge, not through God's salvation.

GOD:	Confucius believed that there was no God, but he was deified in the early 1900s.
FIGUREHEAD:	Confucius
AFTERLIFE:	Confucianism is all about life here on earth. Confucius believed in heaven, but it is not an important part of the religion. Heaven is real but the focus of the religion is earthly.
WORLDVIEW:	Atheistic
SACRED TEXTS:	The Wu Jing or The Five Classics, which is made up of five books of ancient teachings.
	The Analects, which might be called the Confucian bible because it has a collection of sayings by Confucius. Here's a quote: "Hold fast to what is good and the people will be good. The virtue of the good man is as the wind; and that of the bad man, as the grass. When the wind blows, the grass must bend."
WORSHIP SERVICES:	In temples and at family shrines built to Confucius

RITUALS / RITES / SACRAMENTS:	**BIRTH:** The mom-to-be is protected by the "spirit of the fetus." She rests for a month after the baby is born, and her family gives her all the supplies she needs on the 1st, 4th, and 12th months after the baby is born.
	REACHING MATURITY: They don't celebrate this anymore unless the family is really traditional. Basically, the person reaching maturity is served chicken for dinner.
	MARRIAGE: There are eight steps to the process, from the proposal to the breakfast the morning after. It's about family and tradition.
	DEATH: The family mourns the death of the loved one and prepares for a funeral, which they all attend. They wave a willow branch that symbolizes the soul of the person who died.
DID YOU KNOW?	Most of the sacred Confucian texts were actually translated into English by Jesuit missionaries to China.
GEOGRAPHIC CENTER:	China
NUMBER OF FOLLOWERS:	6 million worldwide 26,000 in North America

IMPORTANT VOCABULARY:

FENG SHUI: the concept that stuff should go in a certain place in order to achieve perfect balance

EXAMPLE OF BELIEFS IN POP CULTURE:

Crouching Tiger, Hidden Dragon was about the battle between good and evil (yin and yang) and showed a lot of Confucian ethics—loyalty to the state, the need to honor family, etiquette, and honesty.

CELEBRITY:

Michelle Krusiec,
actor on *One World* and *Titus*

THE TRICK:

They believe in yin and yang, so they believe that all the good will be balanced with evil. The goal of this religion is for all people to become supremely good, but the system they've set up means that this will never happen. The better things get, the more evil will have to come into the world to counteract it. It just doesn't work.

Hare Krishna
CHANTING GOD'S NAME

//world religions: section 1//

SHORT HISTORY

You can trace this religion back five thousand years ago to Vrindavana, a village in India. About that time, in that village, a belief in a god called Krishna began to develop. The movement slowly grew. Then, in the sixteenth century, it got a huge boost by a guy named Caitanya Mahaprabu. Nowadays, this guy is thought of as an incarnation of Krishna. Anyway, Caitanya taught that Krishna was the main god, and that if people wanted a relationship with him they could have it by chanting Krishna's name repeatedly.

Later on (about 1960) a dude named Bhaktivedanta Swami Prabhupada came to America to seek new converts to follow Krishna. In 1965 he organized ISKCON (the International Society for Krishna Consciousness).

BASIC BELIEFS

A lot of the beliefs in this religion are similar to those of Hinduism.

THE TRIUMURTI: This literally means "Three Deities." The three "main" ones are Brahma—the creator, Shiva—the destroyer, and Vishnu—god himself.

REINCARNATION: They believe that you go round and round through the cycle of life over and over many times until you're good enough to go and live forever in heaven with Krishna.

KARMA: To understand Karma, you've got to know that in the Hare Krishna belief system, nothing happens by chance. Everything that happens in life is by the direct action of a higher authority.

Krishna followers stick tight to the "Nine Processes of Devotional Service."

1. Hearing about god
2. Chanting god's name
3. Reading about god and hanging out with others who believe in him
4. Serving Krishna
5. Worshiping god by preparing food and bringing others to see him
6. Praying
7. Encouraging others to chant god's name
8. Developing a close relationship with god
9. Giving everything to god

HOW DOES A HARE KRISHNA BECOME A HARE KRISHNA?

Krishna churches accept anyone, and they recruit mostly through their books that they give away. Interested persons are invited to visit a Krishna temple. Once someone decides to become a member, they have two options. First, if they're interested in becoming a devotee, they can go and live in a Krishna temple with other followers. Or, if they don't want to move into a temple, they are given the title "congregational member" and are allowed to live outside the temple. However, followers are strongly encouraged to move into temples.

WHAT'S THE ATTRACTION?

Getting connected with Krishna here on earth (through chanting) or someday in person in the spirit realm.

WHAT'S THE GOAL?

Trying to break the cycle of reincarnation in order to return to the kingdom of God. Hare Krishnas refer to this as being liberated from the material world. When they get to heaven the goal is to be eternal and loving servants of Krishna.

HOW DOES IT LOOK LIKE CHRISTIANITY?

They believe in one God. They believe Jesus lived.

HOW IS IT DIFFERENT FROM CHRISTIANITY?

Well, they don't believe Jesus was God.

They believe in reincarnation.

GODS:	Krishna—this is the guy in charge of it all. He's the head god. But, there are thousands of other demigods that have different responsibilities.
FIGUREHEAD:	Currently, the power of the ISKCON is divided up between eleven people who run the organization from various parts of the world.
AFTERLIFE:	Reincarnation until you break the cycle and go to heaven to serve Krishna
WORLDVIEW:	Monotheistic with heavy emphasis on pseudo-polytheism
SACRED TEXT:	The Bhagavad-Gita
WORSHIP SERVICES:	Hare Krishna worship is different than anything you might have experienced. Members are not only required to chant sixteen times each day at set times, but they are also required to chant at their worship services. They listen to preaching at their worship services too.
RITUALS / RITES / SACRAMENTS:	**CHANTING:** Krishna followers gain oneness with Krishna through chanting his name. They say it repeatedly, varying the order of different words and stuff like that. Doing this brings peace and tranquility and power here on earth. **FOUR PILLARS OF THE SINFUL LIFE:** Krishna followers believe that not eating meat, staying away from illicit sex, avoiding drunkenness, and not gambling help their spiritual life. Believers are encouraged to honor these rules their entire lives.

RITUALS / RITES / SACRAMENTS:	**APPEARANCE:** Krishna followers have a unique look and style of dress. Women wear saris; men who have devoted their lives completely to Krishna (monks) wear a robe called a dhoti. The monks also shave their heads, leaving a ponytail at the back of their heads called a sikah. Krishna followers sometimes mark up their body's with tilak (a colored substance), or with the names of God.
	NEW NAMES: People who become devoted followers are given new names.
DID YOU KNOW?	The dot between the eyes, called a bindi, indicates a woman is engaged. If she is married, in addition to the bindi, she colors her part on her head red with kunkuma powder.
GEOGRAPHIC CENTER:	Los Angeles, USA
NUMBER OF FOLLOWERS:	More than 1,000,000 worldwide

IMPORTANT VOCABULARY:

KRISHNA: "The All Attractive One"

HARE: the energy of God

RAMA: the greatest Pleasure

VEDAS: the bible of the Hare Krishna religion

ISKCON: the International Society for Krishna Consciousness, established in 1965.

SIKAH: the patch of hair their monks don't shave

DHOTI: the robe a Krishna monk wears

SARI: a skirt that female followers wear

SCENE 1

EXAMPLE OF BELIEFS IN POP CULTURE:

Until 1992, you could be confronted by Hare Krishna followers in airports. They'd offer you all kinds of free things to read. But in 1992, the courts ruled that they weren't allowed to give their material away in airports any longer.

 ## CELEBRITY: ★

The late George Harrison, a former member of the Beatles, showed interest in Hare Krishna. He donated a mansion to the religion and included a Krishna chant in a song.

THE TRICK:

Although Hare Krishna followers seek to uphold good moral principles (the Four Pillars), their works will not bring them eternal life. Christians, too, have the Ten Commandments to follow, but their salvation is not dependent upon their obedience to them. If that were so, we would have no hope! Instead, the Christian believes and trusts that God has already accomplished salvation on the Cross.

Hinduism

HOLY COW

SHORT HISTORY

Hinduism is over 4000 years old, and has changed a ton over the years. It started in the Indus Valley civilization—remember that from your World History class? Well, some invaders came in from the west to conquer the area. They sang while they traveled. The songs were called Vedas. This is where Hindu literature comes from. Some of the stuff they talk about in those songs are still done today—like some of the sacrifices to gods, stuff like that. More literature came out of these ideas that talked about the relationships between god and man. They eventually decided that man is born, dies, and is reborn, just like the seasons on earth. The way you get free from this never-ending cycle is to get rid of all your desire or to become fully aware of your self.

Hinduism is a really varied religion though. There's no one set code of morals, no main organization, and not even one clear opinion about god. It's history isn't real clear.

BASIC BELIEFS

Hindus believe in one god—Brahman. But they believe that there are a lot of other gods that are part of Brahman. They also believe that fate directly influences people's lives. Society in India, a primarily Hindu nation, is controlled by a caste system. There are definite lines between the different social classes—and once you're born into a particular class, you're not getting out of it without a big-time fight.

Hindus also believe that people are reincarnated after they die; what you come back as is determined by your actions here on earth. That's called karma. So most Hindus are vegetarians—you wouldn't want to eat your Uncle Leo in your hamburger at lunch. They view cows as sacred—they definitely don't eat them.

If you achieve enlightenment while you're in your life here on earth, you go to nirvana when you die. There are four kinds of yoga Hindus can practice to become enlightened—these include both meditation and physical exercise.

Hindus are tolerant of other religious beliefs. As long as you're a sincere believer of an authentic religion then you're good to go. This is because they think no one religion (including Hinduism) teaches the only way to salvation. All souls will eventually be saved because everyone is moving closer to union with god in this or some other life.

FOLLOWERS ARE CALLED:
Hindus

HOW DOES A HINDU BECOME A HINDU?

There are three ways you can be saved—
WORKS, KNOWLEDGE, or DEVOTION.

1. You have to follow all the religious rites without messing up,

2. you gain knowledge until you come to a state of mind where karma has no effect, or

3. you become extremely devoted to the gods, your family, and your boss in your public and private life.

WHAT'S THE ATTRACTION?

You can "choose-your-own-adventure" through this religion. There are a lot of gods, so you pick the one that represents whatever issues are important to you at the time. Plus, everyone will eventually be saved—that's appealing.

WHAT'S THE GOAL?

Joy—be satisfied with your income, be happy with your friends, live a moral life, and become spiritually enlightened.

HOW DOES IT LOOK LIKE CHRISTIANITY?

They outwardly believe in a concept of one god.

HOW IS IT DIFFERENT FROM CHRISTIANITY?

They believe in hundreds of other gods that are part of Brahman. And they don't believe in sin.

GODS:	There are many gods to worship, but they are actually all just different aspects of the one supreme being—Brahman. Krishna is the most widely worshipped god. And the Hindu Trinity is made up of Brahma, Vishnu, and Shiva.
FIGUREHEAD:	Think Mahatma Ghandi
AFTERLIFE:	Once you get enlightened you go to a state of nirvana, before that, reincarnation.
WORLDVIEW:	Polytheistic
SACRED TEXTS:	The Hindu scriptures have been written over a period of 2,000 years, and there are quite a few—you've probably heard of the *Vedas, Upanisads,* and *The Bhagavad-Gita.*
WORSHIP SERVICES:	In a temple
RITUALS / RITES / SACRAMENTS:	Prayer and offering rituals should be made three times a day—either at home or at a temple. They also have other yearly festivals and the optional pilgrimage.
DID YOU KNOW?	India makes more movies than any other country in the world because of its many cinematic tributes to gods and goddesses.
GEOGRAPHIC CENTER:	India
NUMBER OF FOLLOWERS:	860 million worldwide 1 million in the USA

IMPORTANT VOCABULARY:

MANTRAS: repeated prayers

GURU: one who is liberated in this life

VEDANTA: philosophy and spiritual practice of the religion

SCENE 1

EXAMPLE OF BELIEFS IN POP CULTURE:

Apu from *The Simpsons* is portrayed as a Hindu. He believes in reincarnation: Krusty tells him, "You only live once." Apu responds, "Speak for yourself." He also meditates, believes in pluralism (lots of religions are okay), and is a vegetarian.

CELEBRITIES:

Madonna. In her video for the song "Music" she morphed into a six-armed Hinduesque figure, dressed as a Hindu priestess at the 1998 VH1 awards, and wore mendhi (Hindu body art) in her video for "Frozen."

Uma Thurman's father named her after a Hindu goddess.

THE TRICK:

If we can work our way to god on our own—through works, knowledge, and devotion—then why do we need god in the first place?

And if you believe in reincarnation, how do you explain the significant growths in population? If new babies being born are using the souls of people who die, is no one making it to nirvana? Are more souls just being created?

Islam and Muslims are all over the news these days. We hear about them a lot, especially since the attacks in New York City and Washington, D.C. on September 11, 2001. But who are these people, really? Lots of people have pointed out that the people who attacked the World Trade Center aren't really Muslims; they're a radical political version of Islam. Well, this chapter talks about the majority of Muslims. The next chapter talks about the Taliban, which are Muslim extremists.

SHORT HISTORY

Remember Abraham, that Old Testament guy, father of the Jews? He had two boys—Isaac and Ishmael. Isaac's kids ended up becoming Jews. Ishmael's became Arabs, who became Muslims. So that's where it all started.

Muhammad is the guy that started this whole religion. He worked for a wealthy woman named Khadija as a trade caravan driver in Mecca, a city in Western Arabia, around 600 A.D. When he was twenty-five, he got married to Khadija, who was forty. They lived together for ten years, and then he started going out to a cave for some alone time. He was bummed out by how the people were worshiping all kinds of idols.

Muhammad was all about uniting the Arabs into one religion. One time while he was in his cave, he claimed that an angel (Gabriel) brought him some revelations from God. The angel told him God wanted him to be a prophet. This totally freaked him out. He didn't write down any of what Gabriel said ('cause he was illiterate), but he memorized it all. When he went home and told Khadija, she believed him and encouraged him to pursue it.

Now, he got a lot of grief about everything he had experienced from the people in town—most of the bigwigs were really threatened by it all. So Muhammad and his followers pretty much had to move out, and they went to a city called Medina. This is a huge event in Muslim history—it's the year Muhammad declared himself to be a prophet of Allah (God) and the year the Muslim calendar starts.

After a few years, Muhammad and his followers went back to Mecca and conquered it. From then on Islam began to spread like wildfire. Muhammad continued to have visions for the rest of his life, and he propagated his religion with military zeal. But he didn't appoint a successor to follow him—this caused a lot of arguments among his followers and eventually caused Islam to break into two divisions. Muhammad claimed to be god's last messenger on earth.

BASIC BELIEFS

It's simple. "There is no god but Allah, and Muhammad is his prophet." They believe that the only valid view of Christ is the one that's in the Koran, which says that Jesus is the son of Mary and a servant of God, but Jesus is not God.

FIVE PILLARS OF ISLAM:

1. There is no God but Allah, and Muhammad is the messenger of Allah.
2. Pray five times a day facing Mecca.
3. Give charity (2.5% of your money) to the poor.
4. Fast from dawn to sunset during the month of Ramadan.
5. If you're financially able, go on a pilgrimage to visit Mecca.

SIX PILLARS OF FAITH:

1. Believe in one god, Allah.
2. Believe in angels of god.
3. Believe in the books of god.
4. Believe in the messengers of god.
5. Believe in the day of judgment.
6. Believe in fate—Allah has already decided what you will get.

FOLLOWERS ARE CALLED:

THE SUNNIS: Most Muslims are Sunni, so they wouldn't really say they were "Sunni," they would just say that they were Muslim. They developed from the group that believed that any early believer of Muhammad could become a Caliph, which is Muhammad's successor.

THE SHI'A: Around 15% of Muslims are Shi'a. They developed from the group that believed that only Muhammad's direct descendents could inherit the position of Caliph. The Shi'ites dominate the nation of Iran and were led by the legendary Ayatollah Khomeini in the Iranian Revolution.

THE SUFIS: You can be either one of the first two *and* Sufi at the same time. Sufis just want to live a really simple life. They are mystics and concentrate on their spiritual existence. The most famous group of them is the Whirling Dervishes.

ISLAMIC JIHAD / TALIBAN: Read the next chapter on Islamic Jihad and Taliban beliefs.

BLACK ISLAM: Check out the chapter on Nation of Islam and Farrakhanism.

HOW DOES A MUSLIM BECOME MUSLIM?

By saying and believing: "There is no God but Allah, and Muhammad is the messenger of God."

WHAT'S THE ATTRACTION?

It's appealing because of its simple message and creed. There is a definite bonus for men because men are in control of everything and women must submit.

WHAT'S THE GOAL?

To unite people to worship one god

HOW DOES IT LOOK LIKE CHRISTIANITY?

There is only one god and he is to be obeyed. He is omnipotent and omniscient. They believe in angels and the devil.

HOW IS IT DIFFERENT FROM CHRISTIANITY?

Allah is not a personal God. He is far above all men and cannot be known. He wants justice more than he wants love. Allah asks his people to make war against "the infidels," but the God of Christians tells His people to "turn the other cheek." Allah prefers judgment over grace, and power over mercy. He is the source of good and evil.

Marriage is for having kids, so men can have up to four wives and as many concubines as they want. However, if they have more than one wife then they are required to treat them all equally. Women have to obey their husbands, and if they don't, then they can be beaten or physically harmed.

GOD:	There is only one god, Allah. Different languages have different names for him, but Muslims believe that it is all the same god. But, if you're Muslim, the only name you call god is Allah.
FIGUREHEAD:	Muhammad
AFTERLIFE:	Muslims believe that when good people die they go to paradise, and when bad people die they go to hell.
WORLDVIEW:	Monotheistic
SACRED TEXTS:	Muslims read four sacred texts. Three of those are from the Bible: the Torah of Moses, the Psalms of David, and Gospel of Jesus (except their version is not exactly like what's in the Christian Bible). They believe the Bible has been corrupted over time because it contradicts the Koran. The last and final holy scripture is The Koran (or Qur'an)—it is the only infallible scripture.
WORSHIP SERVICES:	Meet on Fridays for an hour—men have to go; women can if they want to. Then men and women pray five times every day on their own or at the mosque. There is no priesthood and there are no sacraments.
RITUALS / RITES / SACRAMENTS:	• pray five times daily, facing toward Mecca • fast during the month of Ramadan from sun up to sun down • make a pilgrimage once in their life to Mecca • tithe money to the poor
DID YOU KNOW?	Muhammad's wife, Khadija, had a close cousin who was a Christian.
GEOGRAPHIC CENTER:	The largest number of Muslims live in Indonesia, but the focus of this religion is in Mecca, which is in Arabia.
NUMBER OF FOLLOWERS:	1.2 billion worldwide 7 million in the USA

IMPORTANT VOCABULARY:

ALLAH: god

MUSLIM: a person who follows Islam

RAMADAN: the ninth month of the Muslim year, when they fast

MECCA: where Muhammad was born, the most holy city.

EXAMPLE OF BELIEFS IN POP CULTURE:

SCENE 1

There was a huge controversy in the Arab-American community when the movie *Aladdin* came out a few years ago. They really felt like the movie stereotyped Arabs and should not have been released.

In the movie *Vertical Limit* the character Kareem is a devout Muslim who helps save the lost climbers. At one point in the movie he rolls out his prayer rug and says that he prays because it's what you do before you die that matters.

CELEBRITY:

Hakeem Olajuwon, professional basketball player.

THE TRICK:

Allah is a harsh god, a god of judgement. His devotees cannot personally know him. Where, then, lies the incentive for following him? The God of Christianity invites those who believe in Him to be loved by Him and to know Him personally.

Islam–Taliban
ALLAH'S ARMY

//world religions: section 1//

NOTE: The war in Afghanistan is still going on at the time of this printing, so the information in this chapter is changing daily.

SHORT HISTORY

   Back in the late 1970s, Russia invaded Afghanistan. A bunch of people were sent to refugee camps in Pakistan. It was here that some students began to interpret Islamic law in a really extreme way—they were called students of the Islamic knowledge movement (or Talibs).

   So then, in 1989 Russia pulled all of its army out of Afghanistan and a certain group of people called the Mujaheedin were in control. One of their leaders and some of his followers raped three Islamic women one day, and the leader of the Taliban students planned to kill this guy and his friends. That's when the Taliban started to grow, and their goal was to get control of Afghanistan and apply the Islamic law (as they saw it) to the government. On September 27, 1996, they took over the capital of Afghanistan, Kabul. One person described the city as having streets "full of young bearded men in black turbans, high on Koran and battle." The Taliban students would run around with whips, beating anyone who they thought was being "un-Islamic."

   When the Taliban took over, they captured their enemies' weapons, so they now have tons of machine guns—you'll see Taliban students holding them in pictures. They are believed to have 25,000 to 30,000 soldiers, 200 tanks, and 12 or so airplanes. They have seminaries where their students can get degrees in terrorism. They are definitely focused on warfare.

Even though the Taliban took over in 1996, the only other country that recognizes them as valid rulers is Pakistan. Some people have thought that Pakistan might have a secret alliance with the Taliban. 15% of Afghanistan is anti-Taliban.

The Taliban version of Islamic law allows them to do things like stone women who are out without a male from their family, or amputate the arm of a thief. This type of justice is done arbitrarily—for example, a woman charged with murder was executed in 1997 even though the family of the murdered man said they forgave her and did not want to press charges. So, because of all these human rights violations, the United Nations threatened to quit sending food and other types of relief unless some things changed in the government.

In 1979 the millionaire Osama bin Laden moved from Saudi Arabia to Afghanistan. (He had been expelled from Saudi Arabia and his family had disowned him.) He told the Taliban that he supported them and wanted their protection—the Taliban highly respects this attitude and has chosen to protect him even when other countries have been asked to turn him over. The Taliban has pledged to restore dignity to the Jihad movement (the extremist Islam) by getting rid of what they call "American tyranny," which is "faithless and atheistic."

In 1999, the U.S. declared political and economic sanctions against the Taliban because they support Osama bin Laden, who is well known for his terrorist plots against America and other western countries. The Taliban offered to talk with the U.S., and bin Laden said he wanted to leave Afghanistan. He ended up staying there.

On September 11, 2001, Osama bin Laden organized the strongest terrorist attack against the U.S. in history. He believed that this was a holy attack against the most evil enemy of Allah in the world—Western civilization. The world soon retaliated by launching a war on terrorism. The whereabouts of bin Laden are unknown—we don't even know if he's dead or alive.

They believe in an extreme interpretation of Islamic law. It's all about justice and punishment if you don't conform perfectly. Here are some of the rules of the Taliban.

ENTERTAINMENT: Music, except for religious chants, is prohibited in shops, hotels, and vehicles, and at weddings and parties. Kite flying is considered "useless" and an obstacle to education. Most hobbies, such as keeping pigeons, also are forbidden.

PRAYER: Failure to pray to Mecca five times a day—a requirement of the Muslim religion—is punishable by imprisonment.

DRIVING: Drivers are prohibited from giving rides to women. Violators are subject to imprisonment.

PREVENTING IDOLATRY: Portraits—paintings and photos—are said to promote idolatry and must be destroyed under the law.

WOMEN AND EDUCATION: The Taliban forbids the education of women until institutions are established that segregate women from men. Informal education of women can be punishable by law. For men, at least a sixth-grade education is required.

GAMBLING: Forbidden and punishable by at least a month in prison.

PUBLIC BATHING: The Taliban closed all public bathhouses for men and women. The Taliban says Islam forbids men and women from publicly displaying their bodies.

WOMEN AND THE TALIBAN:

Women living under Taliban rule are considered victims of human rights violations. The Taliban's strict segregation and gender restrictions have been called "gender apartheid." Here are some of the rules for women:

- Not allowed to work
- Under "house arrest"—may not leave the house without a male family member (even if they don't have one)
- A woman seen with a man who is not a family member faces the death penalty—in 1997 a woman was stoned for being out with a man that wasn't family
- No education—they closed all girls' schools
- No healthcare—this hurts them physically and psychologically
- Must wear a "burqa"—a big piece of thick material that's put over their head and goes all the way to the ground (like if you were going to dress up as a ghost for Halloween or something) with a small slit for eyes and breathing. No high heels or white socks.

FOLLOWERS ARE CALLED:
Talibs

HOW DOES A TALIB BECOME A TALIB?

By joining the army and embracing their ideals

WHAT'S THE ATTRACTION?

These are sold-out, passionate people. Some of their followers are almost bribed into joining up—they go find kids on the streets who have nothing, haven't eaten in days or weeks, and promise them food if they'll go to their school. So you've got these little kids learning how to kill because they want to eat that night.

WHAT'S THE GOAL?

To establish a strict Islamic state in Afghanistan

GOD:	Allah
FIGUREHEAD:	Osama bin Laden Mullah Mohammed Omar, Senior Leader
AFTERLIFE:	Paradise or hell. Suicide bombers are automatically going to Heaven because they are considered martyrs.
WORLDVIEW:	Monotheistic
SACRED TEXT:	Islamic Law found in the Koran, but skewed by their extremist interpretation
DID YOU KNOW?	Some people in the Islamic community do not consider the Taliban to be Muslim, even though it has been promoted by the Taliban as Islamic.
GEOGRAPHIC CENTER:	Afghanistan
NUMBER OF FOLLOWERS:	25,000 to 30,000 soldiers

IMPORTANT VOCABULARY:

JIHAD: holy war

FATWA: a legal opinion, but it can become a bounty on someone's head, like with Salman Rushdie, the famous author.

THE TRICK:

Well, for one, their practice doesn't match up with their scriptures—there's a total gap in their logic there. For example, take a look at these guys who hijacked the planes in America because of their "holy war in the name of Allah"—they were in strip bars the night before. That's totally against their religion. It's politics, it's hate, and it's wrong.

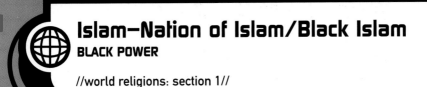

Islam—Nation of Islam/Black Islam
BLACK POWER

//world religions: section 1//

SHORT HISTORY

It all started with the Black Muslim Movement, which was a black urban movement centered on the idea of black superiority. This group (known as the BMM) was started by a guy named W. D. Fard Muhammad. He said that the first humans were black, and that a black scientist created white people in an experiment 6,000 years ago. W. D. Fard Muhammad also taught that white people oppressed black people, and the group focused on the idea of rejecting Christianity. Why? Because the main religion of those white people was Christianity. He also told them that there was no way they could avoid a racial war. This was all going on in the 1930s.

W. D. Fard Muhammad then taught Elijah Muhammad to be a leader, and Elijah eventually took W. D. Fard's place. In the 1960s, another new leader came along—Malcolm X. You've heard of him from the movie, right? Well, he was their most famous spokesperson, but when he heard about Elijah's affairs with other women, he decided to believe in mainstream Islamic faith instead. In 1964 he took his pilgrimage to Mecca. When he went, he realized that the whole idea of hating white people should be changed. Not surprisingly, his idea didn't really go over that well, and he was assassinated.

Enter Louis Farrakhan. He's their current leader and still believes that the black race is better than the white race. He's so well known for his beliefs that some people call this religion "Farrakhanism."

Farrakhanism is different from Islam. People who follow the Nation of Islam and Louis Farrakhan follow the moral law of traditional Islam, but they believe that W. D. Fard Muhammad was god (Allah) in person and Elijah Mohamed (his successor) was his prophet.

Their prophet said that the whites would rule the earth for 6,000 years, and then would be destroyed by the blacks. On judgment day, all the gods (all black, of course) will destroy the white race (devils) and establish paradise on earth. What's it going to be called? Nation of Islam.

THEY THINK:

- God exists, and his name is Allah.

- The Koran is true.

- The Bible is true, but it's been tampered with so much that parts of it are not true.

- Allah sent prophets to give us scriptures.

- Mental resurrection of the dead will happen, and the blacks will have it first.

- Judgment will happen in America.

- Whites and blacks should be separated, and blacks should take the names of the black people of the earth.

- All people should have equal justice.

- White people offering to "integrate" with black people is a deliberate deception, trying to keep the black people from realizing that they should separate from the whites as a nation.

- They shouldn't fight in wars where they'll have to kill people.

- Women should be respected and protected.

- Allah appeared in the person of W. D. Fard Muhammad, and he is the messiah.

HOW DOES A BLACK MUSLIM BECOME A BLACK MUSLIM?

They join the church, but there isn't any clear evidence about how you actually do it.

WHAT'S THE ATTRACTION?

It gives power to people who feel that they've been oppressed.

WHAT'S THE GOAL?

True freedom and equality for African Americans

HOW DOES IT LOOK LIKE CHRISTIANITY?

A lot of the concepts they talk about are found in Christianity—one god, one scripture, judgment day, resurrection after death—but their take on these is very different from Christians'.

HOW IS IT DIFFERENT FROM CHRISTIANITY?

The focus of this religion is on race, not god. They believe that the black race is god's chosen and preferred race. They believe that god is black.

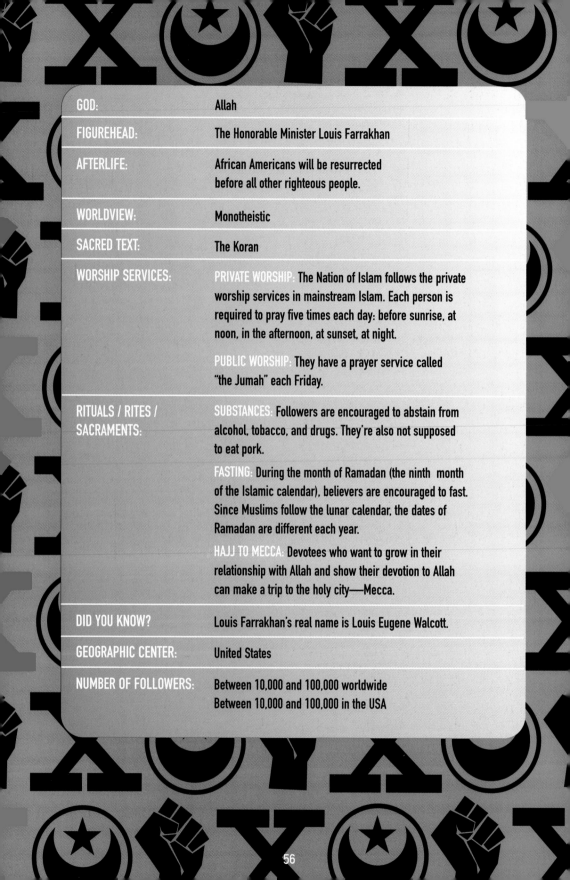

GOD:	Allah
FIGUREHEAD:	The Honorable Minister Louis Farrakhan
AFTERLIFE:	African Americans will be resurrected before all other righteous people.
WORLDVIEW:	Monotheistic
SACRED TEXT:	The Koran
WORSHIP SERVICES:	**PRIVATE WORSHIP:** The Nation of Islam follows the private worship services in mainstream Islam. Each person is required to pray five times each day: before sunrise, at noon, in the afternoon, at sunset, at night.
	PUBLIC WORSHIP: They have a prayer service called "the Jumah" each Friday.
RITUALS / RITES / SACRAMENTS:	**SUBSTANCES:** Followers are encouraged to abstain from alcohol, tobacco, and drugs. They're also not supposed to eat pork.
	FASTING: During the month of Ramadan (the ninth month of the Islamic calendar), believers are encouraged to fast. Since Muslims follow the lunar calendar, the dates of Ramadan are different each year.
	HAJJ TO MECCA: Devotees who want to grow in their relationship with Allah and show their devotion to Allah can make a trip to the holy city—Mecca.
DID YOU KNOW?	Louis Farrakhan's real name is Louis Eugene Walcott.
GEOGRAPHIC CENTER:	United States
NUMBER OF FOLLOWERS:	Between 10,000 and 100,000 worldwide Between 10,000 and 100,000 in the USA

EXAMPLE OF BELIEFS IN POP CULTURE:

SCENE 1

Did you see the movie *Malcolm X*? It's all about the life of the Nation of Islam's most famous leader. And the movie *Ali*, starring Will Smith, is about Muhammad Ali, one of Islam's most beloved members.

CELEBRITIES:

Muhammad Ali, professional boxer and conscientious objector

Malcom X, political revolutionary

Ice Cube, rapper

THE TRICK:

This religion is rooted in the bitterness and hatred of another race. Because these Muslims pick which parts of the Bible they will believe, they conveniently choose to ignore the part about loving your enemy (see Luke 6:27-31). The Bible is God's spoken Word—either it's true or it's not. If they're going to claim any of it, then they need to claim all of it.

Jainism
LIVE AND LET LIVE

//world religions: section 1//

SHORT HISTORY

Jainism is one of the oldest religions in the world. It all started with twenty-four Tirthankara—the guys who started the religion. Lord Mahavira was the last, and he's the one who made the religion what it is today. The first of these Tirthankaras was a guy named Lord Rushabh. They believe that he invented things like marriage, family, law, states, arts and crafts, math, cooking, towns—basically everything that runs our society.

Lord Mahavira was born about 2,600 years ago. He looked around at the culture he was living in and realized that they needed to expand their code of conduct. He did this and implemented it into the daily life of his followers.

Mahavira was a prince. He had anything he wanted at his fingertips. But he wasn't really interested in that stuff. He tried really hard to make sure he never hurt anything. His parents died when he was thirty, and he became a monk. He spent the next twelve years meditating. (Think about that, that's like the time it takes you to go from first grade to twelfth grade!) He went through some really hard stuff during this time—for example, some people came up to him and stuck thorns in his ears. But they say he never had a hard feeling toward those people; he thought that it happened because of bad karma he had from past lives. At the end of the twelve years, he had blocked out (they call it "shaded") all the bad karma and became Keval-Gyan. That's infinite perfect perception of things, infinite perfect knowledge, infinite perfect power, and infinite bliss.

At this point, Mahavira started preaching. He did this for thirty years. He had eleven disciples and organized a structure to the religion. There were monks, nuns, male lay followers and female lay followers. Those four groups combined are called Sangh. It is the supreme body; they are still structured this way today. When Mahavira was seventy-two he fasted to death and got Nirvana (death without being reborn again) and became a Siddha (liberated soul).

BASIC BELIEFS

Jainists believe in compassion, friendliness, and love. They try to watch out for the good of everybody and everything. Literally.

THEY THINK:

- No god exists. However, their founder (Mahavira) was deified after his death.

- You get saved by denying yourself pleasure.

- Practice nonviolence.

- Life involves constant and infinite misery.

- We are helpless in this world. Things, friends, family can't share our trials with us or free us from our fears.

- We are alone. We don't belong to anyone, and no one belongs to us.

- The soul and the body are two totally different things. That's why we shouldn't be afraid.

- The body is dirty and the home of disease.

- We are reincarnated.

Jainism believes that the universe is eternal. It was not created. So, in Jainism, there is no god in the sense of the Creator. An individual is rich or poor, strong or weak, happy or sad all because of his karma. You should be working to stop the flow of karma and shade whatever karma you have in you. You shade the karma through right faith, right knowledge, and right conduct.

When you shade your karma you become a Siddha. This is god. They pray to all Siddha collectively, and not by the names they had when they lived on earth.

The concept of nonviolence is the most important one in Jain. It includes physical as well as mental and verbal violence. The thought of violence is the same as actual violence. Also the concept of nonviolence is for all living beings—plants, insects, animals, or human beings.

All Jains should observe five vows. **Naturally nonviolence is on top of the list.** These vows are:

1. AHIMSA—Don't kill.
2. SATYA—Don't lie.
3. ACHAURYA—Don't steal.
4. BRAHAMCHARYA—Don't have sex. (Women are the cause of different types of evil.)
5. APARIGRAHA—Don't be materialistic.

Jain monks and nuns are not allowed to have any worldly possessions. Jain believers that aren't monks or nuns are allowed to have stuff, but only what is needed. They can't have any attachment to it, and they still have to try to observe all five vows as much as possible. Jains contribute a lot to charity.

FOLLOWERS ARE CALLED:
Jains
Enlightened Jains are called Jinas.

HOW DOES A JAIN BECOME A JAIN?
By following the beliefs, living a life of nonviolence

WHAT'S THE ATTRACTION?
Nonviolence

WHAT'S THE GOAL?
Freedom from attachment to people and things, overcoming karma

HOW DOES IT LOOK LIKE CHRISTIANITY?

Lying and worldly attachments are wrong. Pride is evil, so is killing. They want to be overflowing with love and friendly toward everyone and never ungrateful.

HOW IS IT DIFFERENT FROM CHRISTIANITY?

We don't think it's wrong to kill for food and necessities. (Obviously, Jains are vegetarians.) They are completely works oriented—no grace and no god.

GOD:	None, but their founder was deified
FIGUREHEAD:	Mahavira
AFTERLIFE:	Reincarnation until final liberation
WORLDVIEW:	Atheistic
SACRED TEXTS:	Forty-five Agmas—these are books on math, astronomy, codes of conduct, etc.
WORSHIP SERVICES:	In a Tirth (temple)
RITUALS / RITES / SACRAMENTS:	Navkar Mantra is the most important and sacred prayer. Jains go for pilgrimages to various Tirth (temples) during a year. Some Jain traditions, which don't worship idols, meditate in groups at a special place called Sthanak. It is not necessary to go to a temple or Sthanak to worship. A Jain can worship anywhere as long as he can concentrate.

Six Aavashakya (essentials) are to be performed daily by all Jains. They are:

> **SAMAYIK:** meditation
>
> **CHAUVISSO:** pray and appreciate qualities of the twenty-four Tirthankars
>
> **VANDANA:** respect Sadhu / Sadhavis
>
> **PRATIKRAMAN:** reflect and repent; confess bad thoughts and deeds
>
> **KAYOTSARG:** non-attachment to the body
>
> **PACHCHHAKHAN:** (religious vows) renouncing certain activities for a certain period of time to discipline one's self and increase will power

DID YOU KNOW?	Most Jains are wealthy. Because of their hatred of violence they had to avoid menial labor and do things like finance, commerce, and banking.
GEOGRAPHIC CENTER:	India
NUMBER OF FOLLOWERS:	4 million worldwide 7,000 in North America

IMPORTANT VOCABULARY:

KARMA: It means that whatever you do has a consequence to you. Do a bad thing, get a bad thing done to you. It might not happen to you till later, but it will happen. You can get good karma by doing good deeds and bad karma by doing bad deeds. Your karma "account" determines your existence now and in the next life.

EXAMPLE OF BELIEFS IN POP CULTURE:

Jainists would both support and appreciate the efforts of non-violent groups such as Amnesty International and PETA (People for Ethical Treatment of Animals).

CELEBRITY:

Although **Mahatma Gandhi** was a Hindu, in his autobiography he says he developed his principles of nonviolence not only from Hinduism but also from Jainism.

THE TRICK:

The only way to achieve salvation is to never kill anything (and by that overcome your karma). That is impossible. Every day we kill millions of microorganisms. Salvation is impossible in this religion.

Judaism
WAITING FOR THE MESSIAH

//world religions: section 1//

SHORT HISTORY

The Jews have been around a long time, more than three thousand years in fact. Christianity has its roots in Judaism, and many Christians celebrate their Jewish history.

The story behind Judaism is found in the Old Testament of the Bible. It all started when God told Abraham it was time for him to move. He was supposed to take his family and go, and they didn't know where they were going. God promised that if Abraham would follow him He would bless him, giving him tons of kids and grandkids and making them into a nation—Israel.

So, Abraham believed God, and God gave him a son—Isaac. Isaac had a son, Jacob whose name was changed to Israel. Israel's family moved to Egypt when their country was hit with a famine. There they were made slaves and were supposed to build cities for Pharaoh. They cried out for help to God, and He sent them Moses. Moses led them out in "The Exodus"—that's when they all left Egypt, went to the desert, crossed the Red Sea, ate manna, and all that stuff you've seen in the movie *The Ten Commandments.*

But these guys didn't quite get it. They didn't understand just how awesome God is, and they kept rebelling against Him. He took them to the Promised Land, but they were scared to go in. So God made them wander in the desert for forty years. Lost for forty years. And then, when they got back there again, only few guys had the nerve to go check it out. Finally they entered with Joshua as their leader. After Joshua, they were ruled for many years (like in the hundreds) by people called "judges." During this time they fought a lot of wars and ended up losing and winning some.

When they got tired of all that, they asked God for a king like all the other nations had. God wasn't too keen on that—He was their King—but He gave them what they wanted: Saul. Saul wasn't a great king, and he messed up a lot, so when he died God gave them David. This was one cool guy. He conquered Jerusalem and made it Israel's capital. In the Bible it says he was "a man after God's own heart"; that means that he was in tune with God.

His son Solomon became king when he died, and Solomon built a temple. During his reign Israel became a powerful nation. When Solomon died the kingdom got split in two—Judah and Israel. In 721 B.C. the northern kingdom of Israel was defeated in battle, and in 586 B.C. the Babylonians whipped the southern kingdom of Judah. The Jews were now refugees. The Babylonians destroyed the temple. This meant worship had to change. With no temple left they had to create houses of worship called synagogues. The teachers in the synagogue were rabbis. With the Jews being in exile, their lives changed a lot. They learned Greek and Aramaic, and some didn't learn the biblical Hebrew that everyone knew before. During this time the Old Testament was translated into Greek. This was called the Septuagint.

In 167 B.C. the Jews rebelled and got independence for the Jewish nation. This is what they celebrate now with the festival of Hanukkah. But this freedom was short-lived. In 63 B.C. they were made part of the Roman Empire, and puppet leaders were put in place. This continued during the life of Jesus. In 70 A.D. the Roman general Titus destroyed Jerusalem and the Jews scattered.

When Christianity became a state religion in the Roman Empire in 325 A.D., the Jews were seen as a rejected people and the center of Judaism moved to Babylon. It was more than 1,600 years until the Jews were together as a nation again—in 1948 David Ben Gurion and other Zionists founded the nation of Israel in the Middle East.

Jews believe that God is an omniscient, omnipotent Creator who is present everywhere, and they pray to Him alone. They also believe that the words of the prophets are true, that the Torah will not be changed, that God blesses and punishes, that the Messiah is coming, and that all the dead will rise and exalt God forever.

Forgiveness for sins can be accomplished by **sacrifice, repentance, good deeds, prayer, and God's grace.** Man is justified by strict observance of the law. Jews do not believe in original sin. Man was born righteous and virtuous. They do not believe that Jesus is the Messiah, because He did not bring a world without suffering or political triumph.

SECTS:

ORTHODOX JUDAISM: Observe most of the traditional dietary and ceremonial laws of Judaism, follow the law of the Old Testament.

HASIDIC JUDAISM: These Jews have long beards and sideburns; they walk to the synagogue, etc.

REFORM JUDAISM: The liberal wing of Judaism. Emphasizes religion as a source of ethics. Abraham Geiger (1810–1874) believed that modern people could not accept revelation. Reform Jews believe in the deep-seated sense of kinship within the Jewish people. The hope for a Messiah was fulfilled with the Jewish emancipation. The Torah is a source of ethics to be shared with the world.

CONSERVATIVE JUDAISM: A happy medium between Orthodox and Reform, founded in the nineteenth century.

FOLLOWERS ARE CALLED:
Jews

HOW DOES A JEW BECOME A JEW?

They can be born into the Jewish people, or they can study with a rabbi to convert to the faith.

WHAT'S THE ATTRACTION?

Being a part of a strong and distinct religious history. There's a lot of tradition and celebration in the Jewish faith.

WHAT'S THE GOAL?
Worship God and obey His commandments

HOW DOES IT LOOK LIKE CHRISTIANITY?

Christians and Jews share the same religious history before Jesus. They believe in and worship the same God.

HOW IS IT DIFFERENT FROM CHRISTIANITY?

They do not believe that Jesus is the Son of God; they simply think He was a great prophet or teacher.

GOD:	The God of the Bible, who is the Creator of Heaven and Earth
FIGUREHEAD:	Moses, from the Old Testament Abraham Joshua Heschel, a current rabbi
AFTERLIFE:	Heaven, when everyone is raised from the dead
WORLDVIEW:	Monotheistic
SACRED TEXTS:	THE TORAH: the first five books of the Old Testament THE BIBLE: the entire Christian Old Testament THE TALMUD: a commentary on the Torah, second only to the Bible in importance THE MISHNAH: the oral law
WORSHIP SERVICES:	In a synagogue—involve prayer, singing and chanting, reading of the Scriptures, commentary, etc.
RITUALS / RITES / SACRAMENTS:	THE SABBATH: a holy day of rest, to remember that God created the world and set the Jews free from bondage in Egypt. It's a day of thanksgiving for the many blessings from God. PASSOVER: A feast to celebrate their deliverance from slavery in Egypt (read more in Exodus 12). ROSH HASHANAH: Jewish new year YOM KIPPUR: the day of atonement. Devoted to confession of sins and reconciliation with God and others, a day of fasting. HANUKKAH: eight days in winter. Based on the story of Maccabees in the Apocrypha, these days celebrate the heroic acts of a small group of Jews who overthrew the introduction of worship of Greek gods as a state religion. MENORAH: the eight branched candlestick used during Hanukkah
DID YOU KNOW?	Evan and Jaron, the singing duo, are faithful Jews. They turned down an offer to be the opening act of a big concert tour because they'd have to perform on Friday nights—their Sabbath.
GEOGRAPHIC CENTER:	Israel
NUMBER OF FOLLOWERS:	12 million or more worldwide 6 million in the USA

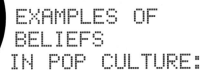

SCENE 1

EXAMPLES OF BELIEFS IN POP CULTURE:

The movie *Keeping the Faith* with Ben Stiller and Edward Norton is about the friendship between a Jewish Rabbi and a Catholic Priest—it spends a lot of time showing what their religious services are like (Hollywood version, of course).

CELEBRITIES:

Dr. Laura Schlessinger, radio personality
Ben Stiller, actor
Jon Stewart, comedian
Adam Sandler, comedian
Ben Stein, game show host and comedian
Dustin Hoffman, actor

THE TRICK:

They believe that Jesus was a great prophet—you either have to believe everything Jesus said (including that He was God) or you have to consider Him a raving lunatic. You can't think He was a good teacher and not believe that He was God—it just doesn't make sense.

Mysticism
DIVINE CONNECTION

//world religions: section 1//

SHORT HISTORY

Mysticism, in one form or another, has influenced many of the world's philosophies and religions, including those in ancient Egypt, India, and Greece. Because it's tied to religions and histories that didn't always keep good records, a lot of the beginnings of mysticism have been lost to historians.

Mysticism goes back to ancient Greece and the school of Philo. He combined teachings of Plato and the Old Testament and taught that by using Plato's teachings and Old Testament facts people could gain access to the mystical god, become one with him, and experience a unity above any unity they'd ever experienced. The next dude who took this idea over was a guy named Plotinus who lived in early 200 A.D. This guy was the first to develop mysticism into an actual philosophical system. He added the idea of monism—the belief that everything in the universe comes from one single source.

From these original roots, mysticism went in different directions. First, Christianity passed its own mystic concepts down through the early church, to the early church fathers. Then, non-Christian religions passed it on too. Pagan cults developed whole religions based on the concepts of connecting with the divine. Even today, religions like Rosicrucianism help promote the concept that we can have a mystical connection with the divine.

BASIC BELIEFS

Mysticism is simple. It's the quest for a connection to the divine. Divine what? Well, that's a good question. Mysticism (in general) doesn't distinguish what god they're after. And, mysticism is more than just a quest. Mysticism is having a knowledge of the divine that may or may not include meditation or contemplation. It seeks to elevate the person and the soul to the divine, so the believer can get to know the divine and become united with that deity.

Through history many different kinds of mysticism have developed. Christian mysticism seeks a connection with God through contemplative prayer and a lifestyle of devotion. Mysticism in general seeks to connect to a source that is labeled "god" through a variety of ways—pagan ritual, witchcraft, or a variety of pagan worships.

FOLLOWERS ARE CALLED:
Mystics

HOW DOES A MYSTIC BECOME A MYSTIC?

Mysticism isn't organized into a religion that you can join. Becoming a mystic means that you go through mystic rituals and adopt the beliefs and practices into your life.

WHAT'S THE ATTRACTION?
Connecting with the divine, an intimate relationship with the creator.

WHAT'S THE GOAL?
Oneness with the divine

HOW DOES IT LOOK LIKE CHRISTIANITY?

Christians can definitely use mystic ideas in their worship of God, so in this area it matches up with Christianity perfectly. But if a non-Christian group is using the principles, then the faith part depends on what that group stands for.

HOW IS IT DIFFERENT FROM CHRISTIANITY?

There are mystical practices from other religions, so if you're into Christian mysticism be careful that you're not getting involved with other religions or cults.

GOD:	For Christian mystics, the Divine is the God of the Bible.
	For non-Christian mystics, the divine is a nebulous, indescribable god usually called Monus—the material or spirit from which everything in the universe was created.
FIGUREHEAD:	None
AFTERLIFE:	They don't all agree.
WORLDVIEW:	Depends on what angle you're coming from
SACRED TEXT:	No one sacred text. Depending on your major religion, you'd follow that text.
WORSHIP SERVICES:	None
RITUALS / RITES / SACRAMENTS:	CHRISTIAN MYSTICISM:
	LECTIO DIVINA: This is one common ritual in Christian mysticism. This is a spiritual practice of reading God's Word and reflecting on it. Monks and nuns have used this for centuries to connect with God and grow deeper in His Word. It involves reading the Scripture, contemplating it, addressing God about what you've read, then communicating to someone in a group about what you've discovered.

RITUALS / RITES / SACRAMENTS (CONT'D):	NON-CHRISTIAN MYSTICISM:
	SPIRITUAL AWAKENING: conscious awareness of a universal force that created everything, and is still around to keep it going
	SELF-EXPLORATION: take off on your journey in the quest to discover the "divine essence of being"
	REMOVING BLOCKS: remove emotional blocks that prevent you from becoming aware of your own divinity
	INTUITIVE DEVELOPMENT: develop your mind in different ways to understand love and god
	SURRENDER: give everything over to the great spirit
DID YOU KNOW?	All major religions including Satanism and Wicca have mystic elements.
GEOGRAPHIC CENTER:	Worldwide
NUMBER OF FOLLOWERS:	We really don't know.

IMPORTANT VOCABULARY:

CENTERING PRAYER: Used by some Christians, it's a type of prayer that focuses more on hearing from God than on talking to Him. It's all about resting quietly in God.

LECTIO DIVINA: Also used by some Christians, it's a way to become aware of God's presence through four steps: *Lectio*, is reading God's Word; *Meditatio* is meditating on the Word; *Oratio* is praying about the Word; and *Contemplatio* is living or resting in the presence of God.

MEDITATION: All religions use some sort of quiet thinking time to focus on the divinity. The ways to do it differ from religion to religion.

EXAMPLE OF BELIEFS IN POP CULTURE:

The movie *Kundun*, directed by Martin Scorsese, is about the life of the Dalai Lama and is a good example of Buddhist mysticism. Also, Gregorian Chants have become popular again recently.

SCENE 1

★ CELEBRITY: ★

St. Augustine. Ever heard of him? He was a monk a long, long time ago who was a Christian mystic. He wrote a book called *The Confessions* that's really famous. ★

THE TRICK:

The focus of this can be the means, not the end—which is the relationship with God. And if the relationship isn't the most important part, then what's the point? Make sure your focus is God, not all the stuff you do to get to Him.

A
Ace
A
A

Rastafarianism
GOD LOVES BLACK PEOPLE
//world religions: section 1//

SHORT HISTORY

Marcus Garvey lived in Jamaica in the 1920s. He was a hugely popular preacher who taught that all Africans would come together and be a powerful group. The Africans compared Garvey to John the Baptist or Moses— leading the people out of bondage and to god. So, who is god? The emperor of Ethopia: Haile Selassie. They called him "Conquering Lion of the Tribe of Judah."

Hmmm, you may say. What's that all about? Well, when he became emperor in 1930, they looked at it as the fulfillment of a prophecy. See, Garvey had predicted that a mighty king would bring justice to the oppressed in Africa. Ethopia is seen as the Promised Land. They believe that all blacks will reunite there. Selassie even reserved a few hundred acres of land for it. He ruled until 1974 then died mysteriously. When he was king he used the name "Tafari." The Ethopian word for *prince* is *Ras*. So you get Rastafarianism.

BASIC BELIEFS

Early in the organization of Rastafarianism, Leonard Howell (one of the leaders) gave it six principles that are considered the main doctrine:

1. Hatred for the white race

2. The superiority of the black race

3. Revenge on whites for their wickedness

4. The negotiation, persecution, and humiliation of the government of Jamaica

5. Preparation to go back to Africa

6. Acknowledging Emperor Haile Selassie as the Supreme Being and the only ruler of the black people

THEY THINK:

- Haile Selassie is the Jesus that the Bible predicts.

- True Rastafarians are immortal.

- Dreadlocks make them look more like Haile Selassie and less like the evil white man. And they believe long hair is biblical.

- They're mainly vegetarians. They definitely don't eat pigs or shellfish. They don't eat anything out of a can or anything that is chemically prepared (like McDonald's). They don't drink sodas—only herbal beverages. They don't season their food.

- Babylon (from the Bible) is white European, western culture.

- Women are subordinate to men.

- Smoking marijuana is a holy sacrament. Marijuana is the key to understanding yourself, the universe, and god.

- Rastas are the supreme race. They're the reincarnations of the ancient tribes of Israel.

- Reggae is the music of their religion.

FOLLOWERS ARE CALLED:
Rastas

HOW DOES A RASTA BECOME A RASTA?

To become a true Rastafarian and adopt the Rastafarian beliefs, you've got to be born black and preferably in Jamaica.

WHAT'S THE ATTRACTION?

Solidarity, especially if you're Jamaican. This religion offers more than just a set of beliefs; it offers unity with fellow strugglers against the white government.

WHAT'S THE GOAL?

Freedom. Overthrow of the anti-black government.

HOW DOES IT LOOK LIKE CHRISTIANITY?

They believe in a god that they call the Lion of Judah. They read from the Bible.

HOW IS IT DIFFERENT FROM CHRISTIANITY?

They believe that god manifested himself in the emperor of Ethopia. They are completely focused on race instead of on a relationship with God.

GOD:	Haile Selassie, emperor of Ethopia. They call him Jah.
FIGUREHEAD:	None
AFTERLIFE:	None. Africa is considered heaven on earth, and true Rastas live forever there.
WORLDVIEW:	Monotheistic
SACRED TEXTS:	The Bible, but only parts that agree with their philosophy. The Holy Piby, a book that's been translated from "Amharic." It speaks of the destruction of the white Babylon.
WORSHIP SERVICES:	There aren't any church buildings.
RITUALS / RITES / SACRAMENTS:	GANJA: also called marijuana. They believe that this was provided by god for them to use for religious purposes. I-TAL: the only kind of food they'll eat. It has never touched any kind of chemical. It's cooked, but served as raw as possible. REASONINGS: a ritual where family members gather for prayers and to smoke ganja BINGHI: all night celebrations. They dance, play rhythms on their drums, and hang out.
DID YOU KNOW?	Haile Selassie was not a Rastafarian. He was a devout Christian and believed that the claims that he was god were ridiculous.
GEOGRAPHIC CENTER:	Jamaica
NUMBER OF FOLLOWERS:	700,000 worldwide

IMPORTANT VOCABULARY

BABYLON: "the system," any state program or office

BALD-HEAD: someone who doesn't have dreadlocks

CHALICE: the pipe they use to smoke ganja

DREAD: someone who has dread locks or someone who is dangerous

ZION: Rastafari Holy Land, in Ethiopia

EXAMPLE OF BELIEFS IN POP CULTURE:

In the movie *Never Been Kissed*, Drew Barrymore's character accidentally gets high with some Rastas at a bar.

Let's get together to fight this Holy Armagiddyon (One Love!), / So when the Man comes there will be no, no doom (One Song!). / Have pity on those whose chances grows t'inner; / There ain't no hiding place from the Father of Creation.

—Bob Marley, "One Love / People Get Ready"

★ CELEBRITY: ★

Bob Marley. He was the quintessential Rasta.

THE TRICK:

You can't "pick and choose" what you want to believe from one source. They believe that Selassie is the Christian God because of some biblical descriptions of the Messiah. But wait, the Bible says that Jesus was the fulfillment of that Messiah! A Rasta would say, "Well, we won't believe that part." It just doesn't work that way!

Romani/Gypsies
WANDERERS

//world religions: section 1//

SHORT HISTORY

Gypsies, more officially known as the Roma, have a history that goes back more than a thousand years. They originally lived in India. Then, about a thousand years ago, they began migrating toward Europe. They've got a very nomadic lifestyle—they're known for always being on the move. And Roma are similar to the Jews in that they are a race (made up of four main tribes) as well as a religion.

There are loads of stories about the history of the Roma. And there are all kinds of tales about their persecution throughout the years. In the fourteenth century, the Roma were used as slaves in Europe. Later, during WWII, they were enslaved in Germany by Hitler. Even now, Roma are oppressed all over the world. Because they are generally stereotyped as lazy, irresponsible thieves, they are often the victims of discrimination in things like education and employment, especially in Europe.

BASIC BELIEFS

They believe in a god named Del, and an evil being called Beng. They use lucky charms, healing rituals and curses. They believe in bixbat, which is bad luck.

A Roma gets three names. The first name is the one you're given by your mother. The second is the one you get when you're baptized. This is the name your other Roma friends would call you. The third name is the one you get later in life. It's mostly used to deal with non-Roma people.

When you die, your family gathers around your dead body and prays for you—they ask forgiveness for the things you've done wrong. They might plug your nose with wax so evil spirits don't enter your body. After you die, you can be reincarnated as an animal or human. They also believe that you can come back as an evil spirit called a muló (also known as the Living Dead).

Romani believe in: loyalty to family, predestination, romaniya, a moral code that changes among the four tribes.

THEY THINK:

- Good luck charms help fight against powers of bad luck.

- Marimé is a state of impurity—they can be kicked out because of it

- Pregnant women are unclean

- Newborns are baptized—moms are unclean until this happens.

- In the past they were usually married between ages 9-14. Pre-marital sex is strongly forbidden.

- Baths are not allowed, only showers.

FOLLOWERS ARE CALLED:
Roma

HOW DOES A ROMA BECOME A ROMA?

They're pretty much born into this religion.

WHAT'S THE ATTRACTION?

The community. They're together all the time.

WHAT'S THE GOAL?

One of the main goals of the Gypsies these days is to get their rights back. They feel they've been slighted by people throughout history. Gypsies also love living together. They emphasize community and the preservation of their culture and history.

HOW DOES IT LOOK LIKE CHRISTIANITY?

They believe in one god and one evil power.

HOW IS IT DIFFERENT FROM CHRISTIANITY?

They believe in charms and luck. They don't believe in the God of the Bible. The whole concept of the body being both evil and good is not biblical either.

GOD:	Del
FIGUREHEAD:	None
AFTERLIFE:	Reincarnation
WORLDVIEW:	Monotheistic
SACRED TEXT:	None
WORSHIP SERVICES:	In their caravans. There's not a certain time that they meet to worship; it's just part of their lives.
RITUALS / RITES / SACRAMENTS:	DRABARDI: Roma women practice this art of fortune telling. They don't read the fortunes of other Romani, just of non-Romani.
	DRABARNI: These are women who practice the art of natural healing.
DID YOU KNOW?	April 8 is International Romani Day.
GEOGRAPHIC CENTER:	Europe
NUMBER OF FOLLOWERS:	12 million worldwide 1 million in the USA

IMPORTANT VOCABULARY:

BAXT: good luck

BENG: the devil

BIXBAT: bad luck

DIKLO: the name for the scarves that Gypsies wear

KUMPANIA: a group of Gypsies living or traveling together

MULÓ: ghosts

ZIGEUNERNACHT: the night when four thousand Gypsies were killed. It happened on August 1, 1944.

SCENE 1

EXAMPLES OF BELIEFS IN POP CULTURE:

In *The Hunchback of Notre Dame,* Esmerelda is a Roma. In the song "Love Potion No. 9," the main character gets the potion from "Madame Rue . . . that gypsy with the gold-capped tooth." And in the second season of *Buffy the Vampire Slayer,* there is an episode where Buffy meets up with some Romani.

A
A
Ace
A
A

CELEBRITIES: ★

★ Gipsy Kings, musicians
Django Reinhardt, jazz legend

THE TRICK:

The Roma focus on this life. They're all about being together, telling their futures, healing people. It's all about the here and now. Even their view of death is about this because they believe in reincarnation. There's no focus on a relationship with God. It's all about themselves.

Shinto
ANCESTOR WORSHIP

//world religions: section 1//

SHORT HISTORY

Shinto is one of the oldest of the world's religions and is purely a Japanese religion. It started about 500 b.c. (or earlier), and it was a mix of nature worship, fertility cults, hero worship, and shamanism. Whew. Basically that means its followers took ideas from a lot of other religions, mixed them together, and made a new religion. Its name comes from the words *shin tao*, which mean "the way of the gods."

Shinto has no real founder, no written scriptures, no body of religious law, and only a loosely organized priesthood. Its followers believe that the deities sit back and watch everything that's going on—and every now and then they'll sustain and protect us.

Shintos believe that Kojiki, one of the first celestial gods, told Izanagi and Izanami, male and female gods, to sleep together so that they would create the islands of Japan. They did. Izanagi and Izanami also created the deities governing the wind, water, grains, minerals, and fire and eventually Amaterasu, the great kami of the sun. The Japanese people believe themselves to be the descendants of kami, which are superior beings with sacred power.

A huge part of Shinto is the focus on ancestor worship. They believe that their dead relatives are near them as spirits and able to help them. They worship them just like they worship the deities, because they believe that after physical death a human spirit still lives to become guardians for them. Believers also respect animals as messengers of the deities.

THEY THINK:

- People are good.
- People are divine.
- The emperor is divine.
- Things that are moral help the group.
- They can pray to lots of gods.
- They don't need to be saved because they're good.

THERE ARE FOUR AFFIRMATIONS IN SHINTO— GOOD THINGS THAT YOU SHOULD FOLLOW.

1. TRADITION AND THE FAMILY: tradition is preserved through family.
2. LOVE OF NATURE: nature is sacred, so if you're in contact with it you're in contact with the divine.
3. PHYSICAL CLEANLINESS: they take baths a lot.
4. MATSURI: a festival honoring the spirits.

FOLLOWERS ARE CALLED:
Shintos

HOW DOES A SHINTO BECOME A SHINTO?
You believe what they believe. Most are born into the religion in Japan, but people also convert.

WHAT'S THE ATTRACTION?
Being part of the religion of Japan. Connecting with your relatives.

WHAT'S THE GOAL?
Makoto—sincerity or true heart

GODS:	They have no all-powerful deity, but they believe in kami.
FIGUREHEAD:	None
AFTERLIFE:	Shintos focus on living a good life on earth, and they downplay what happens in the afterlife. When someone dies, their spirit can go live in heaven (where kami live), the other world of Yomi (where the divine females who gave birth to Japan live), Tokoyo (which is thought to be beyond the sea), or "the other world beyond the mountains."
WORLDVIEW:	Polytheistic
SACRED TEXTS:	Kojiki (records of ancient matters) and Nihongi (chronicles of Japan). Neither are believed to be inspired by the gods.
WORSHIP SERVICES:	In shrines
RITUALS / RITES / SACRAMENTS:	They have shrines dedicated to specific kamis. They have a special gateway there for the gods. They wash their bodies before they go near it. When they get there they pray, dance, and make offerings.

RITUALS / RITES / SACRAMENTS (CONT'D):	They have one Ceremony of Great Purification, where the people go through a national purging of their sins. They hold it twice a year, in June and December.
DID YOU KNOW?	In 1945 Shinto was no longer the state religion of Japan; the emperor publicly said that he was just a human, not the descendant of the sun goddess.
GEOGRAPHIC CENTER:	Japan
NUMBER OF FOLLOWERS:	4 million worldwide 6,000 in the USA

SCENE 1

IMPORTANT VOCABULARY

SEIJO: purity
SHOJIKI: honesty
SEIJITSU: sincerity

EXAMPLE OF BELIEFS IN POP CULTURE:

The *Tenchi Muyo* anime series is based on Shinto themes. These movies follow the idea of nature being divine and encourage the honoring of the spirits.

★ CELEBRITY: ★

Steven Seagal, actor, is a Shinto priest.

A
Ace
A

THE TRICK:

They worship a bunch of gods who are not all-powerful. If they aren't all-powerful, how can they really be gods? The real question is, can a god be a god if he isn't perfect? And if he's not really a god, then why worship him?

Sikhism
GOT ENLIGHTENMENT?

//world religions: section 1//

SHORT HISTORY

Punjab, India. Late 1400s. This guy named Shri Guru Nanak Dev Ji founded the Sikh religion. He received a vision from god and was told to preach to people about god's enlightenment. But apparently, this wasn't just any old vision. He disappeared into a river for three days. People looked for him like crazy, but he finally just reappeared (as the story has it). He claimed that he was hanging with god, and god had told him the secret of the universe. So he became a preacher.

When he died, he was succeeded by nine different gurus. The most important of these was Gobind Singh. He came up with the five symbols of identity (see below). When he died, he declared that the holy scriptures of the Sikhs would be his successor instead of another person. This meant that there would be no more revelation from god.

BASIC BELIEFS

Sikhs believe in one god. They think that he is supreme truth and eternal. They believe in reincarnation—which is the idea that we're constantly being born, dying, and being born again. They also believe that self-centeredness is the source of all evil and that a person achieves spiritual enlightenment by god's grace. Sikhs try to get enlightened, not saved.

THEY THINK:

- One god exists.

- Ten gurus lived—they are guides to god's word.

- All people can experience god— there is no caste system.

- Five symbols of identity:

  1. KESH: uncut hair

  2. KANGHA: comb

  3. KARA: steel bangle

  4. KACHCHA: undershorts

  5. KIRPAN: short sword

- Equality: Everyone is equal before god. This means that women can preach to men and lead prayers.

Sikhs don't dis' other religions, and they don't think they've got the only true way to get to god. They don't try to get people to convert.

FOLLOWERS ARE CALLED:
Sikhs

HOW DOES A SIKH BECOME A SIKH?

Through the Amrit ceremony. The person makes some vows: don't smoke or drink, don't cut hair, don't eat sacrificed animals, no sex outside of marriage, and wear the five symbols.

WHAT'S THE ATTRACTION?

Equality—no one is more important than anyone else

WHAT'S THE GOAL?
Enlightenment

HOW DOES IT LOOK LIKE CHRISTIANITY?

They believe in one god. They believe that god acts out of grace.

HOW IS IT DIFFERENT FROM CHRISTIANITY?

Their god is different from the Christian God. They believe you must follow the five symbols of identity. They don't believe in salvation but in enlightenment. They believe in reincarnation.

GOD:	Waheguru
FIGUREHEAD:	Ranjit Singh
AFTERLIFE:	None, you're reincarnated
WORLDVIEW:	Monotheistic
SACRED TEXT:	*Granth Sahib* or *Adi Granth*; it's written by the gurus.
WORSHIP SERVICES:	In temples called gurdwaras. They bow to their scriptures as an act of reverence. They sing songs. They pray either together or privately.
RITUALS / RITES / SACRAMENTS:	PRAYERS. Sikhs get together several times a day and recite prayers together. MORNING PRAYERS: Two long prayers written in their bible. Each takes about thirty minutes. EVENING PRAYERS: A prayer for after work. The prayer takes about twenty minutes. BEFORE GOING TO BED: A hymn prayer that takes about five minutes.

RITUALS / RITES / SACRAMENTS:	**VAISAKHI:** A Sikh spring festival that commemorates the founding of the Khalsa (the core group of Sikh believers). It's the beginning of the Sikh New Year.
	KHALSA: the baptism of a Sikh into a higher level of membership. Anyone can become a member of the Sikh religion, but not everyone goes through the simple Khalsa (baptism ceremony).
DID YOU KNOW?	Fiber optics were invented by a Sikh. And Sikhs are really involved in helping to fight AIDS.
GEOGRAPHIC CENTER:	India
NUMBER OF FOLLOWERS:	22.5 million worldwide 500,000 in North America

IMPORTANT VOCABULARY

ANAND KARAJ: a Sikh wedding. It's considered a blissful occasion.

DASVANDH: the required 10% tithe

GURU: a teacher, god, or the Sikh scripture

MAYA: delusion. It's a central idea in Sikh beliefs. They teach that everything in this world is an illusion. Someone who is attached to Maya is delusional, and will never break free from the reincarnation cycle.

NAAM: the divine name of god

In *Loser*, when Paul is hitting on Dora in the cafeteria, there is a Sikh sitting behind them studying. And in *The English Patient*, a Sikh helps the two lovers out. There's a Sikh taxi driver in *Rush Hour*.

SCENE 1

★ ★ CELEBRITIES: ★ ★

When we called the Sikh headquarters, they told us that there was a Sikh boxer in Canada who's starting to make it big, and there are also a couple of Sikh models who have kept their turbans on in photo shoots. Look for them in magazines!

THE TRICK:

The whole reincarnation idea is just really hard to believe. Why? Well, more people are being born all the time and the world's population is growing. But if souls just die and come back, where are all the extra souls coming from? New ones? And are no souls being enlightened and going to Nirvana? It just doesn't make a lot of sense.

Taoism
HARMONY

//world religions: section 1//

SHORT HISTORY

Little is known about the founder of Taoism. Some say he was born in 604 B.C., others say 570 B.C. Some say he was born old, with white hair, a long white beard, and wrinkly old skin. Others say his mom named him Plum-Tree-Ears 'cause he was born under a plum tree and had long ears. (Imagine trying to get a date with a name like that!) But his followers just call him Lao-Tzu, old philosopher. Apparently he worked for the Chinese government as a curator of the imperial archives.

But Lao-Tzu soon was disgusted with the mean rulers and the idea of government itself, so he quit. He believed men should live simple lives without a hierarchy of honor and without trying to gain a bunch of knowledge. This idea was pretty cool to a lot of people, so he began to have followers because of his ideas. So to get away from the fame he tried to leave the city, but at the border the guards wouldn't let him pass. They told him that his teachings were so great that he had to write them down to share with others, and until then he could not pass.

So Lao goes home and spends three days writing all he knows. He comes out with a little book called the *Tao te King* or *The Way and Its Power.* No one is sure what happened to him. One story says that he got on the back of a water buffalo and rode off into the sunset never to be seen again. Another says that the guard read the little book and decided to go with him. Either way, no one ever saw him again.

Taoists do not focus on life after death. Instead they work out practical ways to live as long as they can so they can be immortal. Here are a few of their beliefs:

THE TAO: literally means "the way" or "path." It is the way of the universe, the way one should organize their life. You get there by practicing *Wu Wei*, which literally means inaction. We must avoid all aggression by doing things that are natural and spontaneous. We should live passively, avoiding all stress and violence.

THE YIN AND YANG: You've seen it on clothes, skateboards, necklaces, and that kind of stuff. Basically the yin-yang symbol represents the tension between good (yin) and bad (yang) things in the world. It goes a little something like this:

YIN	YANG
Male	Female
Positive	Negative
Good	Evil
Light	Dark
Life	Death

In Taoism, yin and yang are positive and negative principles of the universe. One cannot exist without the other, and they often represent opposites. As you have more and more yang, eventually yin will appear to balance it out, and vice versa. As you travel around the circle, white or black will increase, until the opposite color is almost gone, but never totally gone. The cycle then repeats for the opposite color.

WU WEI: literally means "without action." It's one of the main concepts from Taoism. It means that you make something look easy so that it seems like you're not having to work hard at doing something. By following Wu Wei, you are closely following "the way."

HARMONY: Harmony can only be achieved by looking at the world turned upside down.

GOVERNING: the government should follow "the way" in governing the people as well. Specific chapters in the *Tao te King* describe the ideal way of governing people. They can be summarized in these key points:

- Do not emphasize status, intelligence, or possessions.
- Govern with the least amount of visibility and with a serving attitude.
- Reduce laws and govern lightly.
- Take few actions that involve the people.
- Treat other countries nonaggressively.

THREE CHARACTERISTICS THAT TAOISTS CHERISH:

1. Compassion: leads to courage
2. Moderation: leads to generosity
3. Humility: leads to leadership

FOLLOWERS ARE CALLED:
Taoists / Daoists

HOW DOES A TAOIST BECOME A TAOIST?
By believing what they say is true

WHAT'S THE ATTRACTION?
Keeping peace with everyone

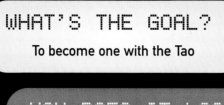

WHAT'S THE GOAL?

To become one with the Tao

HOW DOES IT LOOK LIKE CHRISTIANITY?

They have some of the same morals, like peace and love.

HOW IS IT DIFFERENT FROM CHRISTIANITY?

Denial of God. They deify people, but don't believe in God.

GOD:	None. They deify a lot of people.
FIGUREHEAD:	Lao Tzu and Chang Tzu
AFTERLIFE:	They focus on achieving immortality; but if they do die, they return to the Tao.
WORLDVIEW:	Atheistic
SACRED TEXT:	The *Tao te King* or *The Way and Its Power*— a book that says government should rule by nonaction.
WORSHIP SERVICES:	In a temple
RITUALS / RITES / SACRAMENTS:	DEATH: when a middle-class Chinese person dies, they are given a three-day funeral with Taoist dancers. They do different things to make sure the person doesn't get held up with the gods (their ancestors) on their way to heaven, like burn a death certificate and play music.
DID YOU KNOW?	Taoist priests invented Kung Fu thousands of years ago because they weren't allowed to carry weapons.
GEOGRAPHIC CENTER:	Taiwan
NUMBER OF FOLLOWERS:	20 million worldwide 30,000 in the USA

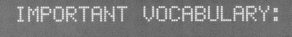

SCENE 1

EXAMPLE OF BELIEFS IN POP CULTURE:

Tai Chi—you're seeing it everywhere lately. Commercials, health clubs, etc. It's a Taoist method for good health. It's about controlling your breath, purifying it, and helping your body in the process.

★ CELEBRITY: ★

Christian Bale, actor, has been trained in Tai Chi.

THE TRICK:

Taoism is about becoming deified and achieving immortality. Basically, Taoists place the notion of a god on themselves, rather than submitting to the authority of the one true God, the Creator of their souls.

Vedanta
SUPREME WISDOM

//world religions: section 1//

SHORT HISTORY

Vedanta has its roots in ancient India. Thousands of years before the birth of Christ, the sages there discovered the truths of Vedanta—that god is one but is called different names by different religions, that god can be known, and that our true nature is divine.

In recent times, Swami Vivekananda—a brilliant young student in Calcutta, India—was asking the religious teachers he met, "Sir, have you seen god?" When he asked Sri Ramakrishna, Ramakrishna replied, "Yes, I have seen god. I see him as I see you here, only more clearly. God can be seen. One can talk to him. If one cries sincerely for god, one can surely see him." Ramakrishna spoke from experience. As a young man, he had an unending desire for union with god, a desire so strong that even things like eating and sleeping became unimportant to him. He was rewarded with the direct vision of god. He sought god through different religions, and as he continued his pursuit of god, he would experience extremely high states of consciousness—states of communion with god—in which truths were revealed to him. Through these moments he realized that every religion, including Christianity, all had the same purpose. All of them sought god. Therefore all religions were worthy and good. Sri Ramakrishna began teaching young Indian men and women what he found.

Swami Vivekananda became one of Sri Ramakrishna's closest students and friends. In 1893, Swami came to the United States as a representative of Vedanta. He was hugely successful. He traveled throughout the United States and lectured about Vedanta, and started the first Vedanta centers.

Since the work of these two, the Vedanta religion has been growing. Its growth isn't huge and phenomenal. It's been quiet, and fueled by lots of Vedantist teachers.

BASIC BELIEFS

Vedanta is more a philosophy than a religion. It's a philosophy that's very practical. In other words, you'll not find a lot of stuff that doesn't "work" here, not a lot of impractical ideas.

The word *Vedanta* comes from two Sanskrit (Indian) words. *Veda* (means "wisdom") and *Anta* (means end—as in "the last word"). So, Vedanta means "supreme wisdom."

- GOD: He's one being. He doesn't need any other being but himself. He can assume any form to convey his presence.

- HUMAN NATURE: Not in need of saving—we're not lost! God is in us, and our nature is divine. Religion is a creation of humans who are on the search for the divine that is in them. Humans are part of a divine, cosmic consciousness.

- APPROACHING GOD: All religions attempt to get to him—all are correct. It's important to respect all religions since they're all on the same quest—to find god, and to discover god in us. How do we connect with god? Lots of ways.

- **EXPERIENCING GOD:** God can be known—when we find god, we feel immense bliss, peace, and love.

- **REINCARNATION:** Humans are born over and over and over and over to complete their work on earth.

- **KARMA:** This is the belief that you create your own future. You cause your own pain. You're the author of your own suffering. How? Through doing kind or hurtful things to others. When you do something bad, you leave a little mark on your consciousness. Through time, whatever you've done will come back to you.

FOLLOWERS ARE CALLED:
Vedantists

HOW DOES A VEDANTIST BECOME A VEDANTIST?

An interest in the teachings is enough to get started. You have to be really interested in the teachings of Vedanta and attend some classes for awhile before you can become a member.

WHAT'S THE ATTRACTION?

Meditation. Finding god inside you. Finding true peace and joy. Discovering a higher plane of consciousness. Attraction to a nonexclusive Indian philosophy.

WHAT'S THE GOAL?

To realize and manifest your divinity

HOW DOES IT LOOK LIKE CHRISTIANITY?

They believe in one god that we can know personally.

HOW IS IT DIFFERENT FROM CHRISTIANITY?

They accept other religions as valid. They believe in karma and reincarnation over grace and salvation.

GOD:	God is within you. He's also higher consciousness, pure existence, and bliss.
FIGUREHEAD:	Vedanta centers each have a swami, a Hindu monk who has taken final monastic vows and leads the congregation.
AFTERLIFE:	Heaven is not permanent. After death, we may spend some time in heaven, after which we reincarnate to finish our work here on earth. To break the cycle of reincarnation and attain eternal freedom is the highest goal of Vedanta—this is done by knowing who we really are and rising to god-consciousness. This can only be done as a human being.
WORLDVIEW:	Theism
SACRED TEXTS:	THE VEDAS: there are four: Rig-Veda, Sama-Veda, Yajur-Veda, Atharva-Veda. They include the Upanishads. The Rig-Veda is the oldest existing scripture on earth. Other scriptures: the Bhagavad Gita and theVedanta Sutras.
WORSHIP SERVICES:	In a temple or in a small shrine in one's own home. The style of worship changes a lot from group to group.

RITUALS / RITES / SACRAMENTS:	YOGA: the main sacrament in Vedanta. Yoga exists for one purpose: to channel the energies that you have to help lead you to god. The word yoga in Sankrit means "yoke" and signifies the union between the soul and god. There are four of these kinds of yogas, and it's best to do all of them and keep each in a "harmonious balance" in your life.
	BHAKTI YOGA: cultivate a loving relationship with god through prayer, ritual, and worship. Through this humans are turned inward to search for the god that's in there.
	JNANA YOGA: reason. You understand god and get freedom through understanding that god is everywhere. Through this yoga you see god in everything—both good and bad events, moments, and emotions.
	KARMA YOGA: service. You get to know god and help others through this kind of yoga.
	RAJA YOGA: meditation. Through this kind of yoga you get to know god through concentration—thinking intensely about god, until your mind is raised to god's level.
DID YOU KNOW?	The Vedanta organization has its own hospitals, maternity wards, nurse training centers, schools, and colleges in India.
GEOGRAPHIC CENTER:	India
NUMBER OF FOLLOWERS:	No one's sure the exact number of people that are involved in Vedanta, so, here's what we know. They've got thirteen "societies" in the United States, and there are also more than 1,000 centers that are related to Vedanta.

IMPORTANT VOCABULARY

AVATAR: an incarnation of god. It's the belief that at many points in history god becomes a human being to point the way back to god. Vedantists look at Jesus Christ as an Avatar.

BHAGAVAD GITA: one of the Vedanta scriptures. The word literally means, "song of god."

GURU: spiritual teacher. Someone who teaches us how to find god.

KUNDALINI: the special power that's inside everyone. How does it come out? Through the four different yogas in Vedanta.

MAYA: a "cloud" that obscures our view of god within ourselves. Without Maya in us, we'd fully recognize our godlike personality.

MANTRA: a short sacred prayer or formula used in meditation.

SANSKRIT: the ancient language of the Vedas (the holy books of Vedanta).

SCENE 1

EXAMPLE OF BELIEFS IN POP CULTURE:

The Legend of Bagger Vance, starring Will Smith, Matt Damon, and Charlize Theron, is based on the Bhagavad Gita, a Vedanta scripture.

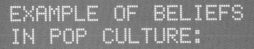 ## CELEBRITIES:

Uma Thurman, actor, and Sting, musician, are both regulars at a chic yoga studio in New York. Madonna has worked Vedanta ideas into her songs.

 ## THE TRICK:

If we are divine, then we are gods. And if we are gods, we have to be perfect in every aspect, including being all-knowing. So their argument that we're gods and just don't realize it doesn't hold up. We aren't gods; we'd know it if we were.

Zoroastrianism
GOOD VS. EVIL

//world religions: section 1//

SHORT HISTORY

Zoroastrianism began with an ancient prophet called Zarathushtra (hey, his name is Zoroaster in Greek—get it!? Zoroastrianism!). He was an Iranian prophet who lived about 1500 B.C. He was born at a time when there was loads of evil in the world, lots of pagan gods. **When he was thirty he had visions of the "one and supreme god" he called Ahura Mazda.**

As opposed to some of the evil deities people were worshipping, the "one god" Ahura Mazda was all good and stood opposed to all the evil in the world, and it was Zarathushtra's job to tell people about Ahura Mazda. How'd he do it? **Songs.** He wrote a lot of songs telling people all about how Ahura Mazda is the all-knowing, eternal god of creation. He was the "lord of wisdom." Through these songs, Zarathushtra told everyone that they should worship Ahura Mazda because he was good.

However, Ahura had an evil counterpart—**Anghra Mainyu.** Zarathushtra taught people that Ahura knew all about this bad guy, and that he knew that he could whoop up on him if he wanted. So, Ahura had this plan—create a world that would trap Anghra Mainyu. It was called the "Seven Creations." He knew that Angra would be attracted to this world, and would fill it with all his evil.

So what does that mean for man? They're in the middle of this fight (like kids whose parents are fighting for custody.) Man has to decide which path he wants to follow, like a kid decides which parent he wants to live with. Zarathushtra taught that people should choose Ahura Mazda and should fight against Anghra Mainyu. How? Through seven qualities known as the Amesha Spentas (hang tight, we'll list these below). If mankind would live these, Zarathushtra believed that evil would be defeated.

BASIC BELIEFS

Man is on a personal quest to get rid of evil and promote the good spirit of Ahura Mazda. He's also on a quest to protect and respect the seven creations: sky, water, earth, plants, cattle, man, and fire. Fire is especially significant because it's considered the source of light, warmth, and life. Man should enjoy (without overdoing it) the gifts that are on the earth. Followers should lead a good, prosperous, and healthy life.

A savior will be born of a virgin, of the line of Zoroaster. This person will raise the dead and judge everyone.

FOLLOWERS ARE CALLED:

Zoroastrians

HOW DOES A ZOROASTRIAN BECOME A ZOROASTRIAN?

They can't convert; they've got to be born into the religion.

WHAT'S THE ATTRACTION?

Living a good life. Understanding the struggle between good and evil. Since you're born into the religion, your family and community share your beliefs.

WHAT'S THE GOAL?

The furtherance of good, the opposition of anything evil, and the final defeat of evil when the world will be made perfect once again, undying and eternal.

HOW DOES IT LOOK LIKE CHRISTIANITY?

They believe in good versus evil. They also have a belief that their savior will be born of a virgin.

HOW IS IT DIFFERENT FROM CHRISTIANITY?

The savior is born of the line of Zoroaster. The god they worship is Ahura Mazda, not God.

GOD:	Ahura Mazda
FIGUREHEAD:	Zarathushtra, or Zoroaster
AFTERLIFE:	When you die, your soul is judged. After that, it gets either a reward or a punishment depending on how you lived on earth. If your soul is found righteous, it goes to the "abode of joy and light." If it's found wicked, it goes to the "abode of darkness and gloom," i.e. hell. But, since there's no eternal damnation in Zoroastrianism, time in the gloomy place is temporary. A series of saviors will come to redeem the lost. And, when Ahura Mazda comes and time ends, each soul will be judged again. Eventually everyone will spend eternity with Ahura Mazda.
WORLDVIEW:	Monotheistic
SACRED TEXT:	The Avesta
WORSHIP SERVICES:	In a Fire Temple. There are no idols.
RITUALS / RITES / SACRAMENTS:	Those who want to live for Ahura Mazda must perfect themselves like the Amesha Spentas (aka the Bounteous Immortals). The seven ideals are: GOODNESS • THE GOOD MIND • TRUTH POWER DEVOTION • PERFECTION • IMMORTALITY They sum up these seven ideals into three, easily remembered ideas called the "threefold path," which members are dedicated to do: "Good thoughts, good words, good deeds."
DID YOU KNOW?	Zoroastrianism is the first nonbiblical monotheistic religion.
GEOGRAPHIC CENTER:	India, but they're originally from Iran (ancient Persia) before the Arabs came there.
NUMBER OF FOLLOWERS:	150,000 worldwide 5,000 in North America

IMPORTANT VOCABULARY:

AMESHASPAND: the highest spiritual beings created by Ahura Mazda. They have attributes of god.

FIRE TEMPLE: the place where Zoroastrians worship

SATUM: a meal offering ritual prayers for the dead

FRESHO-KERETI: The making fresh of the world

EXAMPLE OF BELIEFS IN POP CULTURE:

Gore Vidal wrote a book called *Creation* where he talks about Zoroastrianism, "My grandfather in *his* seventy-fifth year used to talk for hours . . . he was Zoroaster, the prophet of Truth."

★ CELEBRITY: ★

Freddy Mercury from the band Queen

THE TRICK:

If they think we're all going to be saved anyway, what's the use in trying to live by all these rules?

SECULAR WORLDVIEWS

Back to Webster's. What's a worldview? "A comprehensive conception . . . of the world especially from a specific standpoint." That's a lot of big words. Basically it's saying that it's the way you look at the world. Note: not the way you look at God, gods, or goddesses. It's the way you look at this world. That's why you can have one of these worldviews and also follow one of the world religions at the same time.

Agnosticism

WE'LL NEVER KNOW

//secular worldviews : section 2//

?

SHORT HISTORY

The first person to use the word *agnostic* was a nineteenth-century **scientist named Thomas Huxley**. He was from England. Huxley was trying to find a word that described his belief in the world and how he saw it. So, he used the ancient word *gnosis*, which meant "a higher knowledge," and added an "a" before it. Adding the "a" before the word made it negative. So, "a-gnosis" meant that Huxley was on the search to explain that there probably wasn't a higher power or a higher truth that explained the world. He didn't say "definitely." The word mutated into the word *agnostic*.

The discussion about the existence of God has been shaped by lots of people. Here's the basic question on the table for these guys: What can we know? Can we know things that we can't see, or is the only truth that's knowable the stuff that we can see?

Here's the deal. Agnostics believe that it is impossible for us to know if God exists. It's not like they just haven't decided what they think on the matter. They believe we can never know.

Within the whole agnostic philosophy there are smaller groups of different kinds of agnostics:

AGNOSTIC BELIEVERS: These are people who believe that God exists, but they say that there's no way we can begin to know who this God is or what He's like.

AGNOSTIC ATHEISTS: These are people that are almost definitely sure that God does not exist. They'd never say, "I'm for sure that God doesn't exist." They come very close to saying that, but stop just short of it.

FOLLOWERS ARE CALLED:
Agnostics

HOW DOES AN AGOSTIC BECOME AN AGNOSTIC?
They just have to believe what they say.

WHAT'S THE ATTRACTION?
It's really attractive to people who like a good intellectual debate. And since they believe we can't know, the debate can go on forever.

WHAT'S THE GOAL?
Trying to understand if God exists

HOW DOES IT LOOK LIKE CHRISTIANITY?

They think about God a lot, but they don't know if He exists. So, they really don't have any thoughts about what God's like. There aren't any beliefs to share.

HOW IS IT DIFFERENT FROM CHRISTIANITY?

They don't believe in God (because they don't think they can).

GOD:	None, that they know of (or are willing to admit to)
FIGUREHEAD:	None
AFTERLIFE:	The agnostic believers have a desire for eternal life that is just based on unfounded hope. The agnostic atheists think there's nothing after this life.
WORLDVIEW:	Not theist and not atheist. Agnostic.
SACRED TEXT:	None
WORSHIP SERVICES:	None
RITUALS / RITES / SACRAMENTS:	None
DID YOU KNOW?	Most agnostics who want some fellowship join a Unitarian-Universalist church.
GEOGRAPHIC CENTER:	They're organized all over the world.
NUMBER OF FOLLOWERS:	2.6 million in the USA

EMPIRICAL AGNOSTICS: They believe God may exist, but we can't know anything about Him.

EXAMPLE OF BELIEFS IN POP CULTURE:

"If at all God's gaze upon us fall . . ."
—Dave Matthews, "Seek Up"

★ CELEBRITIES:

Matt Groening, the creator of *The Simpsons*
Sarah McLachlan, singer
Dave Matthews, singer
Uma Thurman, actor

THE TRICK:

The trick in the logic here is that there's no point in believing we can't know. If God doesn't exist—then nothing matters here. If He does exist, then we better believe in Him or we'll get eternity in hell. You might as well believe!

(For proofs of God's existence, look in the *How to Decide* section.)

Atheism
NO GOD!

//secular worldviews : section 2//

SHORT HISTORY

Atheism has been around for quite a while. Starting back in ancient Greece, people said there was no God. It wasn't an attack against Christians; it was a belief against the pantheistic belief system of the time, which taught that there were many gods.

About forty years ago, a woman named **Madalyn Murray O'Hair** founded a group called the American Atheists. She fought very hard (and won) to get prayer out of schools. She also fought to have "In God We Trust" taken off American money, but she lost that one. Since then, atheists in this group have held Atheist Pride marches in state capitals. They say that **"coming out"** is letting your family and friends know that you are an atheist. They fight really hard for separation of church and state. They provide literature and speakers to college campuses. They do a lot to promote their cause.

Madalyn Murray O'Hair has been called "the most hated woman in America." In 1995, she, her son, and her granddaughter all disappeared. It wasn't until the spring of 2001 that their bodies were found, and, as most people imagined, they had been murdered.

Atheists don't believe in anything supernatural—god, devil, heaven, hell. They only believe in this world. That means that after you die, you just stop existing. They think that:

- Morals come from humanity, not from any religious code.They rely on communities to come up with their own moral code.

- Evidence about the world and the universe is to be gained through science. They promote science and seek to aid it in any way possible. Science cannot prove the existence of God. So, there is no God.

- Freedom from Religion: Atheists believe that religion imposes too many restrictions on humanity. Since they're all about freedom, atheists not only reject the concept of God, they also want to get rid of all organized religion.

- Freedom of Information: Atheists believe that more mistakes are made from ignorance than anything else. So, they're all for people of every age having free access to all kinds of information. For example, they're into minors having complete access to information about sex so they can learn about it *before* they make mistakes.

- The cosmos is all there is. It is eternal and self-sustaining.

- Evil is a reality, a necessary part of human evolution, but atheists don't know how to deal with it.

- Man does not have an immortal soul.

FOLLOWERS ARE CALLED:
Atheists

HOW DOES AN ATHEIST BECOME AN ATHEIST?
They've got to believe that God does not exist.

WHAT'S THE ATTRACTION?

You don't have to be responsible to any higher power.

WHAT'S THE GOAL?

Proving that no god exists

HOW DOES IT LOOK LIKE CHRISTIANITY?

Not at all. They don't believe in God, so we don't share any beliefs.

HOW IS IT DIFFERENT FROM CHRISTIANITY?

They believe that God doesn't exist and religion is a waste of time

GOD:	None
FIGUREHEAD:	Madalyn Murray O'Hair, founder of American Atheists Ellen Johnson, current President of the organization
AFTERLIFE:	You stop existing.
WORLDVIEW:	Atheistic
SACRED TEXTS:	Humanist Manifesto I and II
WORSHIP SERVICES:	None
RITUALS / RITES / SACRAMENTS:	None
DID YOU KNOW?	In ancient Rome, Christians were called atheists because they didn't believe in the pantheon of gods.
GEOGRAPHIC CENTER:	United States
NUMBER OF FOLLOWERS:	220 million worldwide 1.6 million in the USA

IMPORTANT VOCABULARY:

DETERMINISM: the belief that every event in the world is caused by natural law

FREETHINKER: a person who forms their ideas about God without looking to religion

EXAMPLE OF BELIEFS IN POP CULTURE:

Gene Roddenberry, creator of *Star Trek* who died in 1991, said he purposefully created *Star Trek* to have a god-free, humanistic view of the universe.

CELEBRITIES:

Woody Allen, actor, writer, director

Janeane Garofalo, comedian and actor

Bill Gates, computer giant

Seth Green, actor

Angelina Jolie, actor

Jack Nicholson, actor

THE TRICK:

You can't see God, right? Ever touched Him? Ever smelled Him? So, why should you believe in Him? That's what atheists believe. They forget one thing, however. They can't see the wind, but they can see the leaves rustling in the trees. They can't see natural gas, but they know that it runs their stove or heater. Truth is, while you can't really see God, you can see His effects. For proofs of God's existence, look in the *How to Decide* section.

Existentialism
MAKE A DECISION

//secular worldviews : section 2//

SHORT HISTORY

The history of existentialism isn't that difficult. Two key thinkers shaped the early thought of existentialism.

Søren Kierkegaard was a major player. He stressed the power of the individual and put the pressure on humans to create their own moral code and decide their own destiny. He also encouraged others to find their own sense of meaning in the world. He believed in God, but he encouraged others to look inside themselves for meaning and purpose in life. Finding meaning meant living. If you're living, you're finding meaning. If you're finding meaning, you're living.

Freidrich Nietzsche took Kierkegaard's ideas and went to the extreme. He totally removed God from the picture and said that meaning and purpose for humans could never be found outside themselves. You might have heard Nietzsche's statement, "God is dead." Well, his belief in the death of God, combined with his existentialist philosophy, led him to teach that humans are left here to discover morals and a purpose without the help or support of any deity.

Other thinkers and writers have contributed to existentialism over the years. Christian and atheist existentialists have shaped the existential arguments throughout history, and that shaping still goes on today.

Existentialist beliefs are simple to explain.
They believe in choice over destiny.
Experience over reason.
OTHER BELIEFS:

- They emphasize the individual.

- They criticize today's society and the goals of individuals (to have a comfortable existence) because they are merely part of the "herd."

- They emphasize human freedom and choice.

- They don't think that human existence can be fully explained by reason or objectivity and so an account of human existence must include passion, emotion, and the subjective.

- They focus on death and its role in human life.

- They emphasize anxiety (about death, meaning, and guilt) and its role in human life.

- They emphasize the dynamic and incomplete instead of the static and complete.

FOLLOWERS ARE CALLED:
Existentialists

HOW DOES AN EXISTENTIALIST BECOME AN EXISTENTIALIST?
They have to agree with the philosophy.

WHAT'S THE ATTRACTION?
Explaining the purpose of humanity. Understanding the existence of mankind.

WHAT'S THE GOAL?

Purpose. Meaning. A study in huge philosophical terms.

HOW DOES IT LOOK LIKE CHRISTIANITY?

Belief that we have a free will to make our own decisions.

HOW IS IT DIFFERENT FROM CHRISTIANITY?

God guides us in our decisions—we're not all on our own. And our decisions don't give us our significance; God does. Existentialism often leads to despair because its followers conclude that life has no meaning.

GOD:	Atheist Existentialists: none (largest group)
	Religious Existentialists: God
FIGUREHEAD:	None
AFTERLIFE:	No position
WORLDVIEW:	Monotheistic or atheistic, depending on the person
SACRED TEXT:	None
WORSHIP SERVICES:	None
RITUALS / RITES / SACRAMENTS:	None
DID YOU KNOW?	The movie *Beetlejuice* is loosely based on some ideas from the famous Existentialist Jean-Paul Sartre's play *No Exit*.
GEOGRAPHIC CENTER:	Worldwide
NUMBER OF FOLLOWERS:	Since there's no membership, it's hard to tell.

EXAMPLES OF BELIEFS IN POP CULTURE:

Forrest Gump is all about a guy whose life is decided by chance, and the events have no long-term purpose. The screenwriter, Eric Roth, claimed that he intended for the movie to discuss Existential ideas.

The sci-fi movie *eXistenZ*, starring Jennifer Jason Leigh and Jude Law, is all about existentialism.

 CELEBRITY:

Teller, from the magicians Penn and Teller, says he's "okay with Existentialism."

THE TRICK:

You exist, right? Good. But what about your existence? Who made you exist in the first place? Do you exist just to make decisions? Is there another way to tell if you exist, or does everything rest on your ability to craft your own future? God created you—that's your proof for existence.

Marxism
JOIN THE FIGHT!

//secular worldviews : section 2//

SHORT HISTORY

Karl Marx was born on May 5, 1818. His father was a lawyer, a Jew, who became protestant. Marx went to college where he read law and majored in history and philosophy. Marx was really into the ideas of this guy named Hegel, who believed in the dialectic system. (This means that by studying something and its opposite you can find the truth of its existence.) In Berlin, Marx belonged to a group of "Left Hegelians" who believed an atheistic and revolutionary version of Hegel's stuff. When he graduated, Marx moved to Bonn, Germany, to become a professor. Left Hegelian views were making their mark in Germany at the time.

Meanwhile, Marx was working as the editor-in-chief of a radical newspaper. The government first imposed double and triple censorship on the paper, and then finally decided to suppress it. Working on the newspaper made Marx think that he didn't know enough about politics, so he decided to study it more.

In 1843, Marx got married to a childhood friend. In 1844 Marx met Frederick Engels and they became best friends. They were both involved with the revolutionary groups in Paris and worked out communism (Marxism). Marx was banished from Paris in 1845 as a dangerous revolutionary. He went to Brussels.

In the spring of 1847 Marx and Engels joined a secret propaganda society called the Communist League. They wrote the most famous communist text, *The Communist Manifesto*, in 1848.

HISTORY (CONT'D)

Marx eventually was banished from Belgium. He was banished from Germany. He went back to Paris, and was banished from there, too. Finally, he went to London where he lived until he died. But while all this banishing was going on, many revolutions were taking place that made him think his philosophy was right.

He started another book called *Das Kapital,* but he got sick and couldn't finish it. His wife died in 1881 and then he died two years later. He had some kids, and they all pursued socialism.

BASIC BELIEFS

Life is a struggle between the rich and the poor. That's what it all comes down to for Marxists. The poor are being oppressed, and they need to fight for their rights. God won't do it for you. Why? They don't believe in Him. (Karl Marx was an atheist.) They believe that capitalism (the way America, and most of the world, works) is evil. It allows the rich to become more powerful than the poor.

Marxists believe the best solution is socialism—where everyone lives in total equality. Standard housing. Standard religion. These will remove our class struggles. THEY BELIEVE THAT:

- There is no morality because morals are determined by the greater society, and morals change according to society's needs.

- *The Communist Manifesto,* written by Marx, says that man shouldn't have any private property. All wealth is distributed equally through taxation.

FOLLOWERS ARE CALLED:
Marxists / Communists

HOW DOES A MARXIST BECOME A MARXIST?
They believe in the Marxist system.

WHAT'S THE ATTRACTION?
If you're poor, it's appealing to think that you could be equal with the rich.

WHAT'S THE GOAL?
Equality for all people

HOW DOES IT LOOK LIKE CHRISTIANITY?

The early church community in Acts shared everything and lived in community. However, in Marxism everything is owned by the government while in the early church there was democratic rule.

HOW IS IT DIFFERENT FROM CHRISTIANITY?

It's atheistic, for starters. And its whole focus is on this life, politics, struggle. There's nothing about salvation or having a relationship with God.

GOD:	None
FIGUREHEAD:	Fidel Castro, President of Cuba Jaing Zemin, President of China
AFTERLIFE:	When you die, it's over.
WORLDVIEW:	Atheistic
SACRED TEXTS:	*The Communist Manifesto* is really important, but not sacred in the same way the Bible is for Christians. All writings by Marx and Engels are really important.
WORSHIP SERVICES:	None
RITUALS / RITES / SACRAMENTS:	None

DID YOU KNOW?	Marx memorized the entire New Testament.
GEOGRAPHIC CENTER:	China. Cuba. North Korea.
NUMBER OF FOLLOWERS:	10 million worldwide

IMPORTANT VOCABULARY:

CLASS CONFLICT: The higher class struggles to keep the lower class down. The lower class is struggling to rise above their status.

DIALECTICS: A method of logic where you try to understand how things work together and how opposites can be in unity.

MONEY: What creates class systems and division in society.

REVOLUTION: In order for any change to take place, the existing power must be overthrown.

SCENE 1

EXAMPLES OF BELIEFS IN POP CULTURE:

In a ton of action movies the bad guys are communists—like *Hunt for Red October, Rocky IV,* and *The Saint.*

★ CELEBRITIES: ★

Che Guevera, Cuban revolutionary
Ho Chi Minh, Vietnamese revolutionary
Leon Trotsky, Russian writer and politician

THE TRICK:

Equality for everyone? It'll never really happen because you have to have someone in charge. Also, the attempts to make everyone equal have usually just made everyone poor. The idea that the poor will be equal to the rich means that the rich have to become poor—there's not enough money for everyone to be rich.

Modernism
ALL ABOUT ANSWERS

//secular worldviews : section 2//

SHORT HISTORY

Modernism started when a bunch of scholars wanted to reinterpret the Bible in the scientific terms of the nineteenth century. Pope Pius X called it *modernism* in 1907. That same year the pope declared modernism to be heretical and required that all clergy in the Catholic church say an anti-modernist oath.

So what was the big deal? Well, there were these two philosophers, Hume and Kant. Hume said that all the knowledge we have comes from our senses—pleasure is the highest good, and **morality is a matter of taste.** Kant said that we aren't able to understand anything that our senses can't break through. If our senses don't get it, we don't either. This is a little confusing, but basically it means that if you can't touch it, smell it, see it, or hear it, then it doesn't exist, or it might exist but you can't understand it.

So, a lot of people wanted to apply these thoughts to their religion. The result was that they decided that most of the stuff they read in the Bible was symbolic instead of literally true. This would be something like Mary's getting pregnant with Jesus even though she was a virgin. **Jesus didn't really rise from the dead;** it's just meant to be symbolic. That kind of thing.

BASIC BELIEFS

Modernists claim that science will help you test your beliefs. It won't be able to give you an absolute answer on anything, but it will help you decide what you think is the right answer. There are no standard truths here. We can only make up our own ideas of what we think is true based on our senses. Since we can't see, feel, smell, touch, or taste God, He doesn't exist. Or if He does, then we can't know anything about Him. The Bible isn't completely true—it's just mainly good literature with a bunch of symbolic spiritual truths.

THEY THINK:

- The supernatural is unknowable.
- We have a "religious" sense (like touch, taste, and sight), and that is where we get our Christian ideas.
- Anything from the Bible that contradicts modernism should be taken symbolically, not literally.
- Your beliefs should be evolving—changing and getting better.

FOLLOWERS ARE CALLED:
Modernists

HOW DOES A MODERNIST BECOME A MODERNIST?
They just believe it.

WHAT'S THE ATTRACTION?
Everything seems to have a logical explanation.

Explaining the universe and
humanity's purpose in the world.

HOW DOES IT LOOK LIKE CHRISTIANITY?

Modernists tend to read the Bible and have a good set of morals, but they don't necessarily believe it all to be true.

HOW IS IT DIFFERENT FROM CHRISTIANITY?

They don't believe the Bible is infallible. They make the human mind more important than God.

GOD:	None that we can know
FIGUREHEAD:	Immanuel Kant or David Hume
AFTERLIFE:	No position
WORLDVIEW:	Atheistic
SACRED TEXT:	None
WORSHIP SERVICES:	None
RITUALS / RITES / SACRAMENTS:	None
DID YOU KNOW?	Christian fundamentalism (belief that the Bible is inerrant and should be read literally) came out of the modernist movement.
GEOGRAPHIC CENTER:	Worldwide
NUMBER OF FOLLOWERS:	81 million in the USA

IMPORTANT VOCABULARY:

SCIENCE: Yeah, you thought this was just about combining vinegar and salt and using it to clean pennies, right? Not in modernism. Here, science means the key to all knowledge. In other words, you can't know nothin' outside science.

REASON: The only other way modernist thinkers say you can know anything. They'll allow you to either use science to prove it, or let you use your brain to think out the reason why something works or exists.

FAMILY: Modernist thinkers look at the family in traditional terms: one dad, one mom, some kids, and maybe a dog.

TRUTH: discovered only through science and reason. Sometimes they allow religion to aid the quest for truth, but they never allow religious beliefs to determine the search for truth.

FORM FOLLOWS FUNCTION: a modern art term. First, you ask: What is the function that we need something to fill? Once you've answered that, then you can *design* something that will fulfill the function you need.

EXAMPLES OF BELIEFS IN POP CULTURE:

Paintings by Salvadore Dali (the guy who paints the melting watches) and movies by Andy Warhol (the guy who painted the pictures of Campbell's soup cans) are both considered modern art.

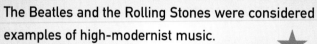

★ CELEBRITIES: ★

The Beatles and the Rolling Stones were considered examples of high-modernist music.

T.S. Eliot wrote modernist poetry.

Frank Lloyd Wright was a modernist architect.

THE TRICK:

If knowledge is based on personal experience of right and wrong, then truth is deprived of any sense of a foundation. Your perception of truth will inevitably differ from another's. So who, then, decides the code for morality? God created a world of order for us to live in, not a world of instability and uncertainty.

Naturalism
IS IT REAL?

//secular worldviews : section 2//

SHORT HISTORY

The history of Naturalism actually has its roots in literature and theater. In the nineteenth century, play sets were often not detailed and actors not exact. Naturalistic theater came along and pushed the acting envelope. Things had to be exactly like they would have been if people weren't watching a play; it had to be totally realistic. From there, writers took the ideas of exactness and applied the ideas of exact science. This leap led to the study of the nature of reality.

What is "real"? Naturalist philosophers concluded that humans were machines. God, if He even existed, was outside the whole creation.

Through history, naturalistic philosophy erupted. It continues to this day, and it is the source that fuels humanism, atheism, and even agnosticism.

They explain life and everything that happens to us in strictly natural ways. That means through science. Okay, look at your hand. Wave at yourself. Give yourself the peace sign. Good. Now, try and explain the movements that you just made from a doctor's point of view. How did all that happen? First, you had the thought. Then, your brain moved that thought to the part of your brain that controls your hand. Then, at an unbelievable speed, a signal is sent to your hand. **Poof. You've got your explanation.**

Really, at its most basic level, naturalism teaches that the universe is basically a machine. It has no soul. It has no desires. It's just a machine. Humans are machines too—without a soul or anything eternal. Here are some of their specific beliefs:

- MATTER: Everything of importance is material. There is nothing that exists that isn't matter.

- HUMANS: You're made up of chemicals and goo. You began as a small fish kind of thing in the water. Over the course of millions of years you left your pool and began to walk on earth. You evolved.

- SOUL / SPIRIT: It's not matter. It doesn't exist.

- SCIENCE: This is the only way you can know anything. Without science you can't know anything.

- YOUR PERSONALITY: You can't see your personality, so how did it come to be? Your personality is the result of matter. It's the result of your brain and your physical being.

- GOD: He's a useless idea. No reason to believe that God exists.

FOLLOWERS ARE CALLED:
Naturalists

HOW DOES A NATURALIST BECOME A NATURALIST?

Naturalism is a philosophical belief system. It's not a religion. You become a naturalist by buying into the belief.

WHAT'S THE ATTRACTION?

It's easy to believe what you see.
It's hard to believe what you can't see.

WHAT'S THE GOAL?

Discovering how we came to be. Trying to explain the origin of the universe.

HOW DOES IT LOOK LIKE CHRISTIANITY?

We both believe that science is real, but Christians also believe in faith and naturalists don't.

HOW IS IT DIFFERENT FROM CHRISTIANITY?

They don't believe in God or the supernatural. They believe that we're only a machine. Christians believe that we're made in the image of God.

GOD:	None
FIGUREHEAD:	None
AFTERLIFE:	When you die, that's it.
WORLDVIEW:	Atheistic
SACRED TEXT:	None
WORSHIP SERVICES:	None
RITUALS / RITES / SACRAMENTS:	None
DID YOU KNOW?	There's a whole film genre that celebrates the naturalist philosophy. What are the rules? Simple. If you're a naturalist actor, you've got to accurately portray the character, scene, and environment as realistically as you can. No special effects, no mechanical alterations, no fantasy. It's all based on reality.
GEOGRAPHIC CENTER:	Worldwide
NUMBER OF FOLLOWERS:	There's no membership, so there's really no way to tell.

IMPORTANT VOCABULARY

FATALISM: Naturalists have a tendency to be fatalists. Fatalists believe that nothing you do in this life matters because it's all predetermined anyway.

SCENE 1

EXAMPLES OF BELIEFS IN POP CULTURE:

The movie *Moulin Rouge* would be the opposite of naturalism—the movie was totally fantastical. Something more along the lines of *The Blair Witch Project* would be how a naturalist movie would look—very real.

CELEBRITIES:

Charles Darwin, evolutionist

Carl Sagan, author of *Cosmos* and the book that the movie *Contact* was based on

THE TRICK:

Some naturalists believe that you don't have a choice in anything. Every thought is predicted. Every one of your actions is predicted. However, they don't believe in God. So who's predicting all of this?

Post-Modernism
ALL ABOUT QUESTIONS

//secular worldviews : section 2//

SHORT HISTORY

In the early 1900s modernism ruled everything. **Science and thinking were the best ways to prove that anything existed.** The culture was like this: Everything could be explained through science and reason. To find out why people acted the way they did, they would make a chart, form a study, have a control group, and get to work. Everything could be discovered in ways like this.

Well, around the 1960s, people began to get a little fed up with this. Why? They began to realize that this whole modern approach to life really wasn't working. Things weren't getting solved that quickly. People were still dying. Life still had many unanswered questions. People began to think outside the scientific box that the world lived in. They began asking questions like "why?" and "how?" without trying to answer them by looking to science or human reason.

Postmodernism tries to understand the absolute outside ourselves. It developed around the idea that the absolute might (or might not) be found. But, however it is discovered, science and human reason can't even come close to grasping it.

140

A basic description of Postmodern ideas is that it's a total denial, rejection, and sprint away from everything that the modern philosophy is. (If you're not sure what that is, go back and read the chapter on modernism). Postmodern thinkers and artists attempt to do everything opposite of the modern philosophy. You'll read all about their beliefs below, but here's the thing: The very basis of postmodernism is that it rejects stereotypes and definitions. So, trying to define this philosophy is difficult—kinda like trying to nail Jello to a wall. Take a look at some of their basic philosophical beliefs:

• HISTORY: Modernism gave facts and figures about the past. Postmodernism seeks to tell the story of history. What were the people like? What did things smell like in the medieval times? They're into telling the story.

• CULTURE: Modernism was all about segregation. Hispanics live in one building. African Americans live in another. Postmodernism seeks to combine cultures. This is called multiculturalism.

• MYTH: In modernism, myths commonly held by cultures were down-played, ignored, and often attempted to be proven false. In postmodernism there's a lot of belief in myths. Instead of ignoring them, postmoderns seek to prove them. They've got total faith in their truth, and have no problem adopting them into their beliefs as truth.

• FAMILY: Alternative family is in. What's that? Gay couples with kids. Single parent households. Any alternative to the "typical family" is accepted.

• KNOWLEDGE: gained through hyperlinks and on-the-fly learning. Knowledge isn't only gained through reading books.

• SEXUALITY: Sexes are joined together and there's little distinction between the two. Androgyny (unable to tell if someone is male or female) is popular and accepted.

• RELATIVISM: Postmodernism applies relativism to everything. Relativism is the belief that truth is relative to the situation at hand.

Postmoderns / Postmodernists

HOW DOES A POSTMODERN BECOME A POSTMODERN?

A lot of it is a generational thing—if you're under thirty-five, you're probably a postmodern. But you just have to believe it.

WHAT'S THE ATTRACTION?

Explaining life. Inclusiveness. Everyone's opinion is equally valid.

WHAT'S THE GOAL?

Explaining things though discovery, mystical practices, and spiritual journeys.

HOW DOES IT LOOK LIKE CHRISTIANITY?

Postmodernism and Christianity look for truth. But they arrive at truth in totally different ways. Postmodernism looks for truth in a variety of places, but Christianity looks for truth in the Bible. Both searches take into account that there's a rational approach and a spiritual approach.

HOW IS IT DIFFERENT FROM CHRISTIANITY?

Postmodernism is an accepting worldview—"different strokes for different folks." It tends to conflict with Christianity's morals at times.

GOD:	No position on God. Depends on the person.
FIGUREHEAD:	None
AFTERLIFE:	Depends upon the person's worldview
WORLDVIEW:	Depends on the person. A postmodern can hold any worldview and be a good postmodern. They can be theistic, pantheistic, atheistic—whatever.
SACRED TEXT:	None
WORSHIP SERVICES:	None
RITUALS / RITES / SACRAMENTS:	None
DID YOU KNOW?	Lots of people think we're getting ready to move into the era of post-postmodernism, if we haven't already.
GEOGRAPHIC CENTER:	Worldwide
NUMBER OF FOLLOWERS:	No membership is necessary, so it's really hard to know. Almost everyone has been exposed to postmodernism.

IMPORTANT VOCABULARY:
None

SCENE 1

EXAMPLES OF BELIEFS IN POP CULTURE:

Did you see that wacky German film *Run Lola Run*? Or movies like *Sliding Doors* or *Groundhog Day* that flip between past and present, showing different outcomes for different decisions? This kind of non-linear story is very postmodern.

 ## CELEBRITIES:

A group like the Beastie Boys, three white guys in a rap band!, or Madonna, with her constantly changing style, are great examples of postmodernism.

THE TRICK:

Go ahead and go on your search for truth. One thing to remember—sometimes you can fall in love with the search and totally miss the person you're searching for. Let God be your search and quest. But don't get so excited about your search that you miss connecting with God.

Secular Humanism
NO WAY OUT

//secular worldviews : section 2//

SHORT HISTORY

Secular humanism is pretty new (as an organized group, that is), but its roots go way back to ancient Greece and China. Basically, people look to humans rather than gods to solve problems.

During the Dark Ages if you wanted to believe something that went against what the church said, you were tortured, executed, or banished from the country. There was a lot of oppression against people who didn't believe the same things as the church. People started to get mad about that, and by the time the Renaissance came around it was acceptable in society to believe in something other than God. Then, by the time of the Enlightenment, everyone was really interested in science, and people started to publicly challenge what the church said. This was called the "free thought" movement.

In America, Mark Twain was a big leader of this movement, and he even got some of the ideas into the Christian churches. Then, in the twentieth century, scientists and philosophers got together to organize a group that believed in humanism. They wanted to provide an ethical system for people without having to believe in a god.

In 1933 the humanists got a document together called *The Humanist Manifesto*. This was like the personal doctrine of their beliefs. They revised it in 1973 and called it the *Humanist Manifesto II*. These days, humanism fuels all kinds of anti-religion stuff. They're actively against prayer in schools (along with many atheist movements), and they're highly anti-religion.

BASIC BELIEFS

The secular humanist doesn't go to God for answers. Basically, you can figure out where they go for answers by looking at their name. Secular *Humanism*. Get the point? If they've got questions about the universe—the problem of evil or whatever—they go to other humans. They use scientific research or other things to solve their problems or answer their questions. They never decide something based on faith.

Secular humanists use science to answer all problems. They want individuals and humans in general to thrive and grow. They are searching for objective truth. They think that the stuff we learn through science constantly changes how we see truth. They want to make this life better for people by helping us understand ourselves and our history. We also become better by understanding what the other people around us think. They're searching for a good code of ethics to follow. And they think that with logic, ideas, good will, and tolerance we can make the world a better place.

The key here is the word *we*. God is not involved. In fact, they don't think He exists. They believe that salvation is a ridiculous idea that man created. They also believe in evolution—again because there's no God.

FOLLOWERS ARE CALLED:
Secular Humanists

HOW DOES A SECULAR HUMANIST BECOME A SECULAR HUMANIST?
They've just gotta believe it.

WHAT'S THE ATTRACTION?

The whole scientific approach.
You get facts for everything you believe.

WHAT'S THE GOAL?

To promote Secular Humanism to the media, public, and government. To provide activities that serve the non-religious community. To research religious and supernatural claims. To educate all levels of people. To show people that their beliefs are viable.

HOW DOES IT LOOK LIKE CHRISTIANITY?

They're trying to make this world a better place to live. Christians would say they're trying to do that too.

HOW IS IT DIFFERENT FROM CHRISTIANITY?

The denial of God. They think they can solve everything themselves.

GOD:	None. Some might say that man is the god of Secular Humanism.
FIGUREHEAD:	A guy named Paul Kurtz is the chairman of the Council for Secular Humanism.
AFTERLIFE:	None. When you're dead, you're dead.
WORLDVIEW:	Atheistic
SACRED TEXTS:	*The Humanist Manifesto I and II*
WORSHIP SERVICES:	None. They often attend Unitarian Universalist churches.
RITUALS / RITES / SACRAMENTS:	None
DID YOU KNOW?	Many secular humanists believe that the Bible is the number one thing keeping women from getting their rights today.
GEOGRAPHIC CENTER:	The Council for Secular Humanism is in New York, but the followers are spread all over the world.
NUMBER OF FOLLOWERS:	12% of the population worldwide 947,000 in the USA

IMPORTANT VOCABULARY:

- **MORALS:** Humanists believe that morals (right and wrong) are created by humans. They don't believe that morals come from God or anything like that.

- **RELIGION:** Humanists say that religion hurts people. All it does is build up their hopes and cause them to trust in a God that really doesn't exist.

- **NIHILISM:** Taken to its ultimate (and depressing) extreme, humanism can lead to Nihilism, which basically says, "Dude, give up—life is meaningless."

- **PROGRESS:** Humanists believe that progress in society happens when humans seek to better their society, and not through the intervention of a supernatural being like God.

EXAMPLES OF BELIEFS IN POP CULTURE:

Spock and Data, from *Star Trek,* always have rational explanations for everything that happens.

And the ACLU (American Civil Liberties Union)—they're fighting for human rights all the time.

CELEBRITIES:

- Albert Einstein, scientist
- Isaac Asimov, author
- Gloria Steinem, feminist
- Marlon Brando, actor
- Helen Keller, writer and inspirational figure

THE TRICK:

Humanists change their concept of truth whenever they find out some new piece of information. It's never the same. Who's to say people aren't just making this stuff up as they go along? They're really quick to give people lists of rules to live by, ways to do things. But they're basing that on people, who change. In order to give someone absolute rules on stuff, you've gotta base your rules on something absolute. And we know the only "thing" that doesn't change is God.

OCCULT RELIGIONS AND PRACTICES

Being part of an occult religion or practice means that you say you have secret knowledge of a supernatural power. And most of these groups want to keep it a secret. They're not real interested in sharing their info with everyone.

Most occult groups have no sense of salvation or redemption—they're just all about playing around with the supernatural. It's like they're into their religion for the kicks, not because they desperately need a relationship with God. It's a game to them. They're playing with fire. And they will probably get burned.

Astrology
STAR-GAZING

//occult religions and practices: section 3//

SHORT HISTORY

Astrology goes back 3,800 years before Christianity became a formal religion. It started with the "Illumination of Bel," the largest astrological work of the Babylonians. Astrology was the original science of the ancient peoples. It was a part of all early civilizations: Chaldean, Egyptian, Chinese, and Indian. Hindus, Buddhists, and pagans all practiced astrology.

The ancient Chaldeans living in Mesopotamia believed the stars were divine beings who decided their fates. The birth of astrology began with the Chaldean priests observing and charting the movement of the stars.

The Chaldeans started the whole watching the stars thing and thus began astrology as we know it. The Babylonians perfected it as an ancient science. As a result, astrology became the number 1 worldview of the day.

The basic belief of astrology is simple. It's the belief that you can watch the stars and predict things. By watching the stars you can know what kind of personality a baby will have when it grows up. By watching the stars, you can know how to solve problems. Through studying the stars you can know what kind of person you should date and marry.

All of astrology runs off something called the "Astrological Chart." This chart is a circle that contains three elements: the Planets, the Zodiacs, and the Twelve Houses. Each of these things is arranged in its own section to cover the whole chart. The planets represent people, the Zodiac signs represent the way each planet (or person) is limited or expanded. The Houses represent different aspects of the human life (like a career or a relationship).

Through the years, astrology has taken on many forms and names. It has become more than just studying the stars. Astrologers believe that the stars predict personality. They've created an entire religious belief system based on it. Astrology has been the major influence in the New Age movement. Its process of divination is strongly rooted in the occult.

WHAT THEY THINK:

- Man and the universe are magically connected. At birth man is somehow connected to and imprinted by the constellations in the universe.

- There are no moral absolutes. Morality is considered to be relative and subjective, thus making astrology amoral.

- The universe and everything or everyone connected to it is divine.

- The universe is evolving.

HOW DOES AN ASTROLOGER BECOME AN ASTROLOGER?

It takes years of practice and training to become one. Using one is simple though. They're all over the place—phone books, new age centers, etc. They're not difficult to find. Using one, though, means that you've probably bought into their occultic ideas.

WHAT'S THE ATTRACTION?

Astrology claims to provide guidance, protect, bring success, tell you the future, and help you understand yourself among other promises. It can tell you what's going on with your soul without demanding you to make any particular moral decision. It fulfills the need for a spiritual connection in a secularized world.

WHAT'S THE GOAL?

- To completely know yourself as well as the future through studying the stars
- To evolve through self-awareness
- To achieve harmony with oneself and the universe

HOW DOES IT LOOK LIKE CHRISTIANITY?

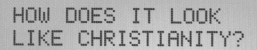

The prophets in the Old Testament were able to see signs from God and warn people of things that would happen in the future—but this was a gift from God, not something they figured out from the stars.

HOW IS IT DIFFERENT FROM CHRISTIANITY?

Christians believe that God is in control of our future, and we can't get clues or predict what will happen in our lives based on the stars. God's Word discourages us from looking to the stars to try to predict our future. The astrologer seeks ultimate meaning from God's creation rather than from the Creator.

GOD:	None. God is seen as an impersonal force. Astrologers do not accept a God who would impose a moral standard of what is right or wrong on man.
FIGUREHEAD:	Dane Rudhyar (1895–1985), pioneer of humanistic and transpersonal astrology Sybil Leek, author Jean Dixon, prophetess
AFTERLIFE:	As many as 75–80% of astrologers believe in reincarnation.
WORLDVIEW:	Pantheistic, occultic, gnostic, or polytheistic
SACRED TEXTS:	The sky. The Astrological Chart.
WORSHIP SERVICES:	None

RITUALS / RITES / SACRAMENTS:	• Read horoscopes
	• Read palms—like your hand
	• Read tea leaves
	• Read tarot cards
DID YOU KNOW?	**Astrology** is looking at the stars and using them to predict everything you can. **Astronomy** is the science of studying the stars and planets. They're totally different.
GEOGRAPHIC CENTER:	Worldwide
NUMBER OF FOLLOWERS:	1 billion 40 million in the USA

IMPORTANT VOCABULARY:

DIVINATION: the process of trying to manipulate something for your own purposes; the concept that you can reach into other worlds and get answers for your own benefit

EXAMPLES OF BELIEFS IN POP CULTURE:

Practically every magazine you pick up will have your horoscope in it. Astrologers have created them from the astrological charts. In one episode of *Will and Grace,* Will goes to see an astrologer who ends up being right about lots of things in his life.

CELEBRITIES:

Shirley MacLaine, actor

Nancy Reagan, former First Lady

Walt Disney, legendary animator

THE TRICK:

Astrology was originally based on the idea that the solar system revolves around the earth. Well, like 600 years ago Copernicus proved that to be wrong. So the whole thing is based on faulty science.

Black Mass
AN UNHOLY WORSHIP SERVICE

//occult religions and practices: section 3//

WARNING: The Church of Satan is a powerful and dangerous religion. As Christians, we believe that the devil is real and is a force of evil. He will be defeated in the last days, but for now he has limited power on earth. We recommend reading this chapter only after praying to be covered by the armor of God found in Ephesians 6 of the Bible.

SHORT HISTORY

The Black Mass was supposedly started in France in the fourteenth century. It grew in popularity in the fifteenth and sixteenth centuries. It's a part of the satanic movement, one of their "worship services."

Black Masses were attended by English Noblemen who thought it was cool to do anti-church things. One very well-known mass took place for the mistress of King Louis XIV. They said the mass three times, then cut the throats of children. Their blood was drained and mixed with flour to make communion wafers. They took communion, then had an orgy. When people found out about the mass, almost 250 people who were involved were arrested—including some of France's highest ranking officials. Some were sent to jail, others were executed.

In the nineteenth century, the Black Mass went into serious decline. Today, the Church of Satan doesn't officially practice it. However, some fringe satanic groups still do. Their masses not only include the backwards Catholic Mass, but they also include things like orgies, necrophilia (having sex with dead people), and drinking human blood.

ople who attend Black Mass are Satanists.

cally, this ceremony is just a parody of a Catholic Mass. It's
ded to make fun of the Mass, make fun of God and Jesus, and
jabs at the Christian religion.

endees of the Black Mass perform the Catholic Mass back-
. They turn the cross upside down and they spit on it—or they
on it. They stab the communion bread. Instead of using Holy
r or wine, they use human urine (yuck), and they'll use rotting
tables or leather for communion bread. The priest performs
eremony and usually wears a robe with an upside down cross
at's head on it.

ey believe that Christ should be ridiculed and Satan
uld be worshipped.

FOLLOWERS ARE CALLED:
Satanists

HOW DOES A SATANIST BECOME A BLACK MASS ATTENDEE?

ttend a Black Mass if you're involved with Satanism;
elieve in Satan and want to worship him.

WHAT'S THE ATTRACTION?

Sensory overload, participation in a mystical ceremony.
A desire to degrade the Christian faith.

WHAT'S THE GOAL?

Worshipping Satan, celebrating sinful desires like lust and greed

HOW DOES IT LOOK LIKE CHRISTIANITY?

It uses all the same symbols, figures, etc., but they're all reversed and desecrated.

HOW IS IT DIFFERENT FROM CHRISTIANITY?

They worship Satan. Christians worship God.

GOD:	Satan
FIGUREHEAD:	None
AFTERLIFE:	Hell
WORLDVIEW:	Monotheistic
SACRED TEXT:	*The Satanic Bible*
WORSHIP SERVICES:	Can be held anywhere, but a Black Mass is the worship service itself.
RITUALS / RITES / SACRAMENTS:	Drink blood. Human sacrifice. Spit on the cross. Have sex with dead people.
DID YOU KNOW?	The Satanic Church now believes that this mass is outd
GEOGRAPHIC CENTER:	The United States
NUMBER OF FOLLOWERS:	Unknown. Some people believe that those who perform Black Mass are getting fewer and fewer in numbers.

IMPORTANT VOCABULARY:

- **BAPHOMET:** an upside down five-pointed star with a picture of a goat's head on it. Often the symbol for Satan used in the Black Mass.

- **SABBATS:** gatherings of witches. Sometimes at these gatherings they hold Black Masses.

- **PRIEST:** Nope, not the guy you might see on Sunday at church. This is a satanic priest who performs the Black Mass ritual.

- **CHALICE:** holds the wine used in a Black Mass.

- **SCROLL:** has the entire mass written on it. Since it's a long mass, it helps to have the stuff you're supposed to say written down.

- **THE KNIGHTS TEMPLAR:** an occult group accused of conducting Masses where they denounced Christ, worshipped idols, spit on the cross and worshipped Satan.

- **GILLES DE RAIS:** a French baron accused of conducting Black Masses in his cellar. He was accused of kidnapping, torturing and murdering over 140 children.

EXAMPLE OF BELIEFS IN POP CULTURE:

Mick Jagger and Keith Richards of the Rolling Stones were asked to appear in a movie entitled *Lucifer Rising.* They declined.

 SCENE 1

★ CELEBRITIES: ★

Marilyn Manson wrote an introduction to *Satan Speaks* by Anton LaVey.

Ozzy Osburn, musician

THE TRICK:

The goal of Satanists is to seek pleasure. The way they do this is to ridicule God, the giver of abundant life. Doesn't make much sense, does it? No wonder Satanists have a really high suicide rate and have always been associated with suicide.

Dowsing
A WEIRD WAY TO FIND STUFF

//occult religions and practices: section 3//

SHORT HISTORY

Depending on who you are, and where you live, you might have heard of dowsing, but maybe not by this name. It's also called divining, water witching and doodlebugging.

What the heck is it? Dowsing is very simple. You hold a Y-shaped stick in your hands—you hold one end of the "Y" in either hand, and let the straight part stick out away from your body. Then you hold it, think about what you're looking for, and walk. Eventually, the stick points to the ground, and you've found what you're looking for.

We're talking about something that's more of a practice than a belief. Dowsing is something that's not been written about a lot, so there's not much detailed history associated with it. Dowsing is thought to have existed as long as eight thousand years ago. Historians have found cave drawings that depict people searching for water using a forked stick. They've found etchings from ancient Egypt of pharaohs using dowsing rods. They've uncovered drawings of Chinese emperors 2,500 years ago doing the dowsing thing, as well as finding evidence of people dowsing as early as 400 B.C. in ancient Greece. It was written about for the first time in the 1650s by a well-known philosopher named John Locke. He claimed that you could find precious metals under the ground by using a dowsing rod.

Since Locke first wrote about this practice, there has been a struggle about what to do with it. Some people just love it, and believe that you really can find water with a dowsing rod. Others think it's just a bunch of hoopla, and that it doesn't work. Some believe it to be an occult power.

People from both sides got together to either prove or disprove dowsing. What happened? Well, that depends on who you asked. In some scientific tests, dowsing failed miserably. In others, it passed.

BASIC BELIEFS

Basically, dowsing is the search for energy fields. It's been used mostly in searching for water. How does it work? It involves something called E-Rays that originate from the earth. These rays send out invisible clues about where things are located. You can detect these invisible fields by using a dowsing rod. How? Well, first you hold the rod with the two branches of the Y in each hand, then you think in your mind what you want the rod to find. Water? Oil? A cheeseburger? It'll find whatever you tell it to. Then, the rod will respond as you walk by pointing down to the thing you're looking for.

Dowsers believe that these E-Rays affect everything from plant growth to the lines that ants make when they walk. So, some dowsing scientists have developed different kinds of machines and devices to measure and detect E-Rays.

In theory, dowsing could be used to find all kinds of things including oil, land mines, buried cash, or anything else that's buried that you might be hunting for.

DOWSING METHODS:

FIELD DOWSING: traditional use, locating water or objects

REMOTE DOWSING: supernaturally locating a target from a distance

MAP DOWSING: the use of a map in locating a target

INFORMATION DOWSING: obtaining information on any subject: a medical diagnosis, a weather forecast, etc.

FOLLOWERS ARE CALLED:
Dowsers

HOW DOES A DOWSER BECOME A DOWSER?
Pick up a stick, hold it correctly, and start walking. It's not an organized religion, so there's no membership.

WHAT'S THE ATTRACTION?
Searching for a treasure.
For some, it'sdeveloping psychic power.

WHAT'S THE GOAL?
To find what you're looking for

HOW DOES IT LOOK LIKE CHRISTIANITY?

Many Christians believe dowsing to be a gift from God and utilize it in their lives. Anyone can dowse, but to be effective one must go into a light trance state, which is a dangerous place to put yourself.

HOW IS IT DIFFERENT FROM CHRISTIANITY?

Dowsing is considered to be a psychic activity. The Bible strictly forbids that kind of stuff.

GOD:	There aren't any gods associated with this. However, many dowsers believe that a demon controls the stick.
FIGUREHEAD:	None
AFTERLIFE:	No position
WORLDVIEW:	Occultic
SACRED TEXT:	None
WORSHIP SERVICES:	None
RITUALS / RITES / SACRAMENTS:	None
DID YOU KNOW?	Dowsing is in the Bible. Where? Hosea 4:12 and Deuteronomy 18:9-12. Dowsing is, without doubt, a form of divination.
GEOGRAPHIC CENTER:	Worldwide
NUMBER OF FOLLOWERS:	Unknown

IMPORTANT VOCABULARY

CURRY LINES: Named after the Swiss physician Manfred Curry, they're invisible lines that run all over the earth.

HARTMAN LINES: Named after the German physicist Ernst Hartman, these invisible lines run north, south, east, and west all over the earth and cross at various points.

E-RAY: also called Erdstrahlen or Earth rays. Invisible and undetectable to the human eye, these are believed to be evil rays. When they cross, bad things happen (like car accidents).

EXAMPLE OF BELIEFS IN POP CULTURE:

Some of the Bugs Bunny cartoons you watched when you were little showed characters walking around with a Y-shaped stick, dowsing.

★ CELEBRITIES: ★ ★

There really aren't any celebrities directly associated with this practice that we know of, however Stephen King is on the www.dowse.com website under an author list. There is a pretty famous psychic named Uri Gellar who uses dowsing to help mineral companies know where to drill.

THE TRICK:

God wants us to trust Him for the things that we need in life. He didn't say in Matthew 6, "Don't worry about the food and drink you need to live, just use a dowsing rod and you will find it." He said that He would provide for us, and we are not to worry! So don't waste your life focusing on all the stuff you can get; trust God and He'll provide for you.

Freemasonry
A SECRET SOCIETY

//occult religions and practices: section 3//

SHORT HISTORY

Freemasonry claims ancient roots for its beginning.
However, most historians and scholars of fraternal organizations consider Freemasonry claims to simply be an attempt at credulity.

The Lodge (Freemasonry) began in 1717 in London. The early adherents of Masonry were **Christian**. However, the Lodge underwent a shift in philosophy and as a result became aligned with the occult. Albert Pike, a leading mason, reworked the system of advancement (degrees) within Freemasonry and introduced much of the occult influences in the organization that continue to rule the Order to this day.

The first Lodge in America was established in 1733 in Boston. Freemasonry quickly grew throughout the nation, and by the late 1800s there were several thousand lodges in the states. It ultimately became the most influential organization in politics and social and religious institutions.

Freemasonry is comprised of several groups. They are the Blue Lodge, The York Rite, The Scottish Rite, The Shrine, and Eastern Star. **Eastern Star was established in 1850** for the purpose of including women **(Mason's spouses)** into an otherwise male-dominated organization.

The secrecy of the Lodge opened it up to criticism and eventually caused its membership to decline.

GOD: Freemasonry attempts to be inclusive and not offensive to a member's religious persuasion, whether a member be Hindu, Muslim, Buddhist, Jewish, or Christian.

SACRED LAW: Masons are required to have some kind of sacred book open at meetings. They can use it at a meeting if they want. The book doesn't have to be the Christian Bible, but it has to be some book that the members of the lodge would feel is holy.

RELIGION: Masons believe that religion is vitally important in the life of the member, but they don't spend any time talking about religion at their meetings.

SOCIAL JUSTICE: Masons are big on helping others—the poor, oppressed, and needy all get help from masons either financially or through direct acts of service.

FOLLOWERS ARE CALLED:
Masons

HOW DOES A MASON BECOME A MASON?

First there are some basics. You've got to be at least twenty-one, you can't have a criminal record, and you have to love America.

After that, you're **required to follow an order.** First you've got to petition any lodge for membership. How do you find a lodge? Ask someone you know who might be a member. Lodges aren't allowed to publicize, so you'd have to ask around. When you submit your application you'll also have to submit three references. From there, the lodge you petitioned will read your application and vote on whether or not to accept you. They'll contact you for an interview, which includes your family. From there, they'll take all the information about you back to the lodge, and they'll vote on you again. If you get voted in you'll be assigned an instructor who will teach you the meaning of the degrees. If you don't get voted in, you lose your application fee.

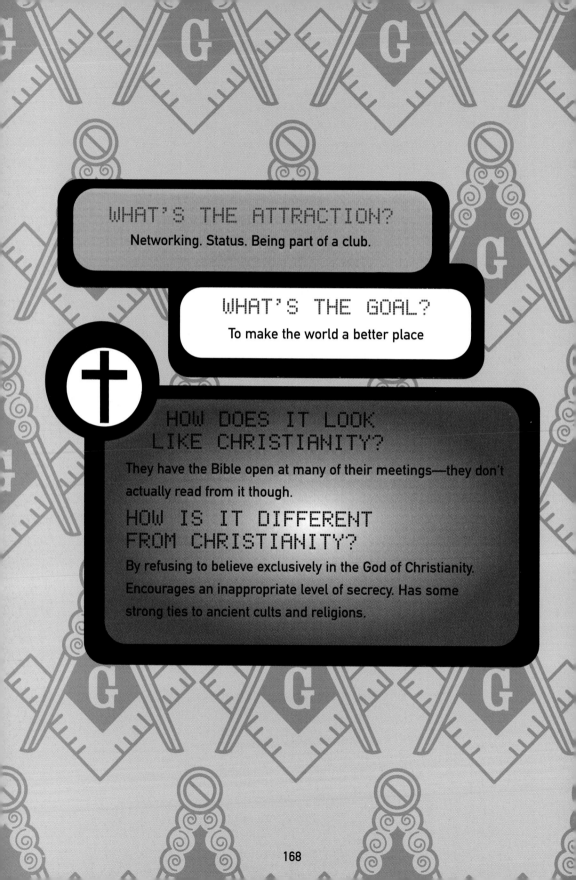

WHAT'S THE ATTRACTION?

Networking. Status. Being part of a club.

WHAT'S THE GOAL?

To make the world a better place

HOW DOES IT LOOK LIKE CHRISTIANITY?

They have the Bible open at many of their meetings—they don't actually read from it though.

HOW IS IT DIFFERENT FROM CHRISTIANITY?

By refusing to believe exclusively in the God of Christianity. Encourages an inappropriate level of secrecy. Has some strong ties to ancient cults and religions.

GODS:	Any God will do in freemasonry. Officially, they state that they believe in one God, and you can call that God whatever name you want. Allah. Yahweh. Bill. Whatever works for you, works for them. but, you have to believe that some God exists. Atheists aren't allowed.
FIGUREHEAD:	Each lodge has their own Worshipful Master who is the head of the lodge.
AFTERLIFE:	No position
WORLDVIEW:	Polytheistic—in that they accept many deities as being relevant Deistic—in that they view God as being outside the universe without personal influence over man's situation
SACRED TEXTS:	They accept a variety of texts as sacred—anything a member feels is sacred is recognized.
WORSHIP SERVICES:	Masons don't worship in their lodges together. They're encouraged to go to church wherever they choose.
RITUALS / RITES / SACRAMENTS:	Shhh . . . they're all secret. Although the organization itself is widely known, there's not a good chance that you're going to hear what their rituals are unless you're a member.
DID YOU KNOW?	Freemasonry and Mormonism have common rituals. Actually, Joseph Smith, the founder of Mormonism, became a Mason in Nauvoo, Illinois, and introduced much of it into the temple ceremonies.
GEOGRAPHIC CENTER:	The United States, Europe, and the U.K.
NUMBER OF FOLLOWERS:	5 million worldwide 2.5 million in the USA

IMPORTANT VOCABULARY:

WORSHIPFUL MASTER: the president of a lodge

SENIOR WARDEN: the Senior Vice President of a lodge

DEGREE: a degree is a level of achievement. Thirty-three degrees is the highest level a member can achieve.

SCENE 1

EXAMPLES OF BELIEFS IN POP CULTURE:

The movie *The Skulls* is an example of a secret society. There's an episode of *The Simpsons* where Homer becomes part of a secret club and gets all kinds of perks. In the movie *From Hell* (starring Johnny Depp and Heather Graham), Jack the Ripper is tied to the freemasons.

CELEBRITIES:

Michael Richards, actor (Kramer from *Seinfeld*)
Buzz Aldrin, astronaut
John Wayne, actor

THE TRICK:

You've got to believe in God, and they allow you to believe in any God. But all these gods make different claims. You can't accept them all because they all disagree.

Hypnosis
YOU ARE GETTING VERY SLEEPY . . .

//occult religions and practices: section 3//

SHORT HISTORY

The word *hypnosis* comes from the Greek word *hypnos* meaning "sleep." It goes back to a guy in the eighteenth century named Franz Anton Mesmer. This dude was interested in all kinds of things. He liked studying astrological stuff. He had a hobby of using magnets to help heal people, which he called Mesmerism. The magnets also induced a sleep-like state in his patients. Mesmerism caught on all over the place, and the guy became famous.

After his beliefs caught on, people began to copy him. One group of people put each other in these similar sleep-like states, but they didn't use any magnets to heal people. It was at this time that people began calling what Mesmer did "hypnosis." A split soon formed between the people who used the magnets, and the people who didn't. Eventually, people who didn't care for the magnets began to form serious study groups around the new concept called hypnosis.

Through the years, hypnosis has been studied as a science, adopted as a tool in counseling, and used in performances at comedy clubs and other shows.

Hypnosis is a state of relaxation and concentration. The process of hypnosis is the attempt to get your mind to completely relax and concentrate. In this relaxed state, your mind will be able to focus on particular issues that it wouldn't otherwise be able to focus on. Many people believe (incorrectly, according to scientific hypnotists) that hypnosis is really a time when you are asleep, or a time when your mind is in an unconscious state. This isn't true. Hypnotists attempt to put their subjects in a relaxed state where the mind is more open to questions or suggestions.

THERE ARE MANY KINDS OF HYPNOSIS:

STAGE HYPNOSIS: This is the hypnosis most people are familiar with. They see this stuff on television or in movies. It's mostly done for show.

CLINICAL HYPNOSIS: This is often used by counselors. After hypnotizing their client, the counselor will make suggestions to help their client overcome problems.

PARAPSYCHOLOGICAL HYPNOSIS: Parapsychologists might use this to gain information about occult matters.

POLICE HYPNOSIS: This is the hypnosis used by police when they need to get information from someone about a crime that they've witnessed.

FOLLOWERS ARE CALLED:
Hypnotists

HOW DOES A HYPNOTIST BECOME A HYPNOTIST?
They take classes to become certified hypnotists.

WHAT'S THE ATTRACTION?

Having control over someone (if you're hypnotizing that person). Getting rid of a bad habit (if you're being hypnotized).

WHAT'S THE GOAL?

That depends on the branch of hypnosis. Hey, look—not everyone wants to be embarrassed by acting like a chicken. Many people use hypnosis to get rid of a bad habit or to gain a new ability.

HOW DOES IT LOOK LIKE CHRISTIANITY?

Hypnosis doesn't look like Christianity at all.

HOW IS IT DIFFERENT FROM CHRISTIANITY?

The Bible says that we should let our mind be like that of Christ Jesus (who never let His mind be put into an unguarded state by a hypnotist, even just for kicks). God also tells us to be alert for any tricks the devil may use to attack us—how can we do that if we're spaced out?

GOD:	Depends on the religion of the hypnotist
FIGUREHEAD:	Frederick Winters and Johnathan Chase
AFTERLIFE:	No position
WORLDVIEW:	No position
SACRED TEXT:	None
WORSHIP SERVICES:	None—therapy sessions would be the closest thing to one
RITUALS / RITES / SACRAMENTS:	None
DID YOU KNOW?	Even when you're hypnotized, you can't be forced to do something you don't want to do, like being told to act like a chicken. It just doesn't happen that way.
GEOGRAPHIC CENTER:	There are hypnotists who have got centers of study and teaching all over the world.
NUMBER OF FOLLOWERS:	It's a safe estimate to say millions of people have used hypnosis.

IMPORTANT VOCABULARY:

AUTONOMIC NERVOUS SYSTEM: the nervous system that keeps your body going without you needing to be conscious

AUTOGENIC THERAPY: a form of self-hypnosis that's done by using six suggestions

ENDORPHINS: chemicals released by the brain to relieve pain

HYPOGENIC: things that a hypnotist might use to put someone in a hypnotic state—like a watch or a necklace

UNCONSCIOUS: where all your memories and emotions are stored. Hypnosis is the quest to discover these memories.

EXAMPLE OF BELIEFS IN POP CULTURE:

In Woody Allen's movie, *The Curse of the Jade Scorpion*, he and Helen Hunt play characters that are hypnotized by an evil hypnotist so that they will steal jewelry and bring it to him.

CELEBRITIES:

Albert Einstein, scientist

Thomas Edison, inventor

Kevin Costner, actor

Jackie Kennedy Onassis, former First Lady

THE TRICK:

Hypnotism is a powerful thing; it really works. But God instructs us to bring "every thought into captivity to the obedience of Christ" (2 Corinthians 10:5, NKJV). Not having control over what enters and leaves your mind is treading on thin ice.

Magic: The Gathering

A HOUSE OF CARDS

SHORT HISTORY

Magic the Gathering is a recent game. A guy named Richard Garfield developed it and then, in 1991, revealed it to the public at a gaming convention. At the convention, the game took off.

Why'd it become so popular so quickly? Two reasons. First, people love to collect things. They especially like to collect cards (remember baseball cards when you were younger?). So, when these well-designed, artistic cards hit the streets, people who collected cards ate them up. Second, it has its roots in fantasy, and people who love fantasy generally love this game. The combination of these two factors has led to this game's widespread popularity.

BASIC BELIEFS

This is difficult, because we're not talking about a religious system, and we aren't talking about a philosophy. Basically, this is a complex way to spend your free time. Depending on who you ask, you'll get the following statements and ideas about the Magic card game:

- "IT'S JUST A GAME." Some people would say that it is just a game. Not any different from spending a few hours in front of the TV or Xbox. The theories and ideas don't reflect or affect their personal beliefs or ideas when they play it.

- "THIS GAME AFFECTS YOUR PERSONAL LIFE." This might come from your parents. The major complaint from some religious groups about this game is that it becomes addictive and takes your eyes off God.

• "THIS GAME IS THE SPAWN OF SATAN." Many people feel the world of fantasy and magic is filled with strong connections to the occult world. They view this card game as the newest attempt by Satan to connect with teenagers and pull them into his world.

The game is set in a world called Dominaria. Each character in the game is called a planeswalker or a mage. The goal is to battle other planeswalkers. There are five powerful forces or elements; each force has a corresponding color.

WHITE means holy, life, light.
BLUE means the power of knowledge.
BLACK means evil and death.
GREEN means the power of life and nature.
RED is the color of chaos, fire and destruction.

Each planeswalker picks one or more forces to associate with each character. As they play the game, their associations with these powers help them win battles.

This is totally a strategy game. You've got to figure out how to make your deck of cards beat the other player's deck of cards. The elements help you do this; so do spells which are attached to elements.

• *Creature* spells are played to make the card's creature do what the player wants.
• *Land* cards show how much power, or manna, a player has.
• *Sorcery* cards allow players to cast spells.
• *Instant* cards let players cast a fast spell.
• *Interrupt* cards are the fastest spells and are only used to mess with another player's spell.
• *Enchantment* cards are continuous spells that don't stop until the game is over.
• *Artifact* cards give power that anyone in the game can use.

These are the basic cards. It's a really complex game with tons of rules that change all the time, but that's the main info you need to know.

FOLLOWERS ARE CALLED:

Magic players

HOW DOES A MAGIC PLAYER BECOME A MAGIC PLAYER?

You buy a deck, practice, get together with another player and play the game.

WHAT'S THE ATTRACTION?

It's a game! Playing a fantastical game offers a sense of the mystical, as well as an intellectual challenge.

WHAT'S THE GOAL?

While winning is important, it is almost secondary to things like improving your deck, utilizing combination cards, refining strategies, etc. The game is like chess in that it requires an understanding of the mechanics of the cards and how they work together. Plus one of the purposes of the game is just to hang out with friends.

HOW DOES IT LOOK LIKE CHRISTIANITY?

Magic has a spiritual element. It deals with negative spiritual forces but deals with them in a different way than Christianity does. Magic the Gathering tends to promote the battle between good and evil, but says that evil has an equal chance at winning. Christianity, however, says that God wins in the end.

HOW IS IT DIFFERENT FROM CHRISTIANITY?

The chance that evil can win in the end. The use of spells. It's a fantasy world.

GOD:	No position
FIGUREHEAD:	Richard Garfield, the creator of the game
AFTERLIFE:	No position
WORLDVIEW:	No position
SACRED TEXT:	None. Their rule book changes quite a bit and tells them how the game is played, but it's not sacred.
WORSHIP SERVICES:	None
RITUALS / RITES / SACRAMENTS:	Playing the game really isn't a ritual, but perhaps it does seem a little like a ritual. We'll give you the general idea of how the game is played, which is not unlike many other types of card games.

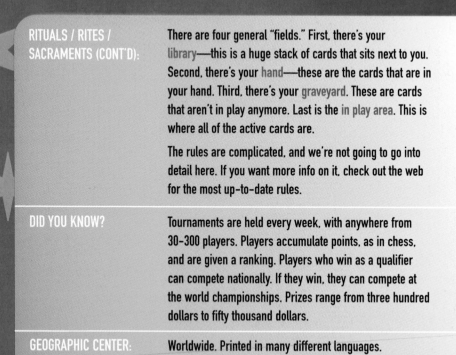

| RITUALS / RITES / SACRAMENTS (CONT'D): | There are four general "fields." First, there's your library—this is a huge stack of cards that sits next to you. Second, there's your hand—these are the cards that are in your hand. Third, there's your graveyard. These are cards that aren't in play anymore. Last is the in play area. This is where all of the active cards are.

The rules are complicated, and we're not going to go into detail here. If you want more info on it, check out the web for the most up-to-date rules. |
DID YOU KNOW?	Tournaments are held every week, with anywhere from 30-300 players. Players accumulate points, as in chess, and are given a ranking. Players who win as a qualifier can compete nationally. If they win, they can compete at the world championships. Prizes range from three hundred dollars to fifty thousand dollars.
GEOGRAPHIC CENTER:	Worldwide. Printed in many different languages.
NUMBER OF FOLLOWERS:	6 million worldwide

IMPORTANT VOCABULARY:

SPELL: Every card that does something is a spell except for land.
POWER: Each player gains power with every game. The higher your power, the more hits you can take in a game.
HITS: The damage inflicted on you during a fight in the game.

SCENE 1

EXAMPLE OF BELIEFS IN POP CULTURE:

ESPN 2 televises the Magic national and world championships.

CELEBRITY:

R. A. Salvatore, an author who writes for Wizards of the Coast, the company that publishes *Magic: The Gathering* playing cards—we don't know if he actually plays the game though

THE TRICK:

Well, you might think it's just a harmless game. God says, "Test everything. Keep what is good and stay away from everything that is evil" (1 Thess. 5:22, NCV). Are spells and magic evil? I'd suggest you stay away from it— even if you don't notice what it's doing to you, it might be subtly numbing you to the heavy darker occult stuff.

Necromancy
I SEE DEAD PEOPLE

//occult religions and practices: section 3//

SHORT HISTORY

Necromancy has many sides and elements to it. Look at it this way: as long as people have existed, they've had a fascination with dead people. They've tried talking to them. They've tried getting them to rise from the dead. And they've tried to get them to do things (whether they stayed dead, or got up and walked around).

Some people believe that necromancy goes back as early as biblical times. Saul got the witch of Endor to conjure up the spirit of Samuel (check out 1 Samuel 28 and see for yourself). But probably the practice of trying to awaken the dead goes back further.

Rewind several hundred years, and you'll see necromancy practiced all over the place, and in every century. The whole necromancy thing got to be big in the United States in the mid 1800s when two sisters, Margaret and Kate Fox, claimed they heard ghosts in their house. They could make the ghost knock on the door by snapping their fingers. Turns out they were lying, but that didn't stop people from looking for dead people. It got more popular through the years, and then, in 1960, a guy named James Pike tried to talk with his dead son. He did this on television. Years later, Pike disappeared in a desert.

People have been trying to contact their croaked friends all over the place. No one's sure if they're talking to their friends, a demon, or are just faking it.

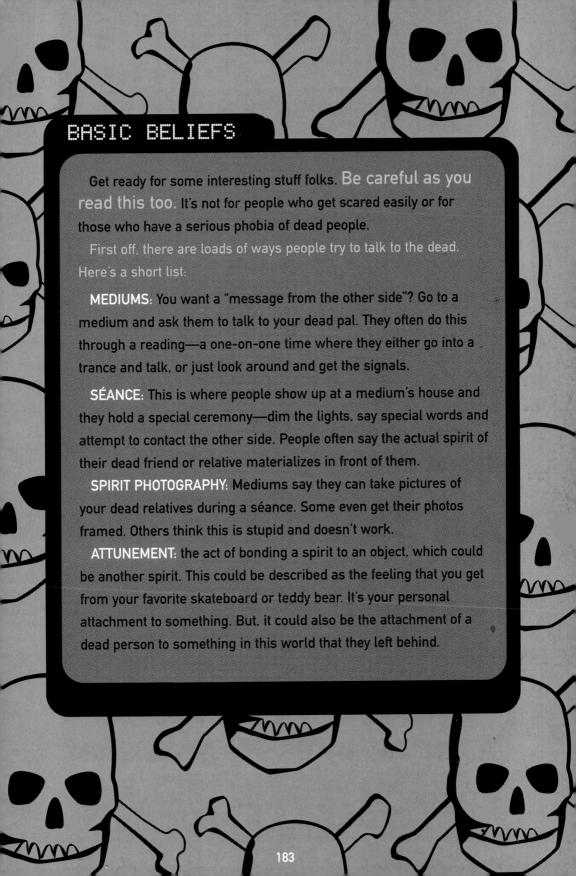

BASIC BELIEFS

Get ready for some interesting stuff folks. Be careful as you read this too. It's not for people who get scared easily or for those who have a serious phobia of dead people.

First off, there are loads of ways people try to talk to the dead. Here's a short list:

MEDIUMS: You want a "message from the other side"? Go to a medium and ask them to talk to your dead pal. They often do this through a reading—a one-on-one time where they either go into a trance and talk, or just look around and get the signals.

SÉANCE: This is where people show up at a medium's house and they hold a special ceremony—dim the lights, say special words and attempt to contact the other side. People often say the actual spirit of their dead friend or relative materializes in front of them.

SPIRIT PHOTOGRAPHY: Mediums say they can take pictures of your dead relatives during a séance. Some even get their photos framed. Others think this is stupid and doesn't work.

ATTUNEMENT: the act of bonding a spirit to an object, which could be another spirit. This could be described as the feeling that you get from your favorite skateboard or teddy bear. It's your personal attachment to something. But, it could also be the attachment of a dead person to something in this world that they left behind.

THERE ARE DIFFERENT DEGREES OF ATTUNEMENT:

Bonding: the second, stronger level of attunement. At higher levels, bonding allows two people or a person and an object to exchange telepathic links letting the other know where it's located and how it feels.

Spirit Locking: The third level of attunement. In this case, people are connected even after death, and can only be released by the person creating the link. (Hint: the person creating the link is called a necromancer).

SPIRIT BONDING: (Get ready for weird!) This is when a necromancer leaves his or her body and possesses the body of someone else. While in the person's body, the two duke it out. If the person who owns the body gets defeated, their spirit is destroyed forever. If the necromancer wins, they've got the opportunity to put the person's spirit in a jar or box, and that person's spirit becomes a genie.

FOLLOWERS ARE CALLED:
Necromancers

HOW DOES A NECROMANCER BECOME A NECROMANCER?

By going to a medium or studying up on it. There are various creepy things you have to learn, such as spell casting and raising the dead. You get this stuff from books and by practicing with a necromancer.

WHAT'S THE ATTRACTION?

Talking to the dead. Having power over spirits. Spell casting.

WHAT'S THE GOAL?

Communicating with the dead. Getting answers. Casting spells.

HOW DOES IT LOOK LIKE CHRISTIANITY?

A necromancer believes in the afterlife, but not the Christian view of afterlife, which is heaven or hell. People might try to convince you of the acceptability of necromancy by referring to Saul's visit to the witch of Endor in 1 Samuel 28. However, the Bible portrays this as a sinful thing.

HOW IS IT DIFFERENT FROM CHRISTIANITY?

A focus on and fascination with the dead. God wants our focus to be on Him, our Creator, not His creation.

GOD:	Depends on the religion of the necromancer
FIGUREHEAD:	None
AFTERLIFE:	They believe that the soul lives on after a person has died, and can be called back up to revisit earth.
WORLDVIEW:	Occultic
SACRED TEXT:	None
WORSHIP SERVICES:	You've gotta ask, "Where do these people get together, hang out, and have a good time?" Think about it! Wherever dead people are. So, Necromancers will often hang out at sites where there's a lot of blood (because blood is seen by the dead as a source of life)—graveyards or battlefields.
RITUALS / RITES / SACRAMENTS:	Seánces. Spirit bonding. Attunement.
DID YOU KNOW?	Hey, necromancers don't consider this Satanism. They don't attempt to talk to Satan. They just want to talk to the dead.
GEOGRAPHIC CENTER:	Worldwide
NUMBER OF FOLLOWERS:	Unknown

IMPORTANT VOCABULARY:

CHANNELING: receiving messages from the dead or from the spirit world

ATTUNEMENT: the practice of binding a spirit to an object. When you manipulate the object, you manipulate the spirit.

SPELLS: something necromancers use to raise dead people. They also use spells to protect themselves from enemies.

SPIRIT PHOTOGRAPHY: Some mediums will say that they can take a picture of your dead relative during a séance.

SPIRIT BONDING: when a necromancer leaves their body and possesses the body of another person

EXAMPLE OF BELIEFS IN POP CULTURE:

In *The Sixth Sense,* starring Bruce Willis and Hayley Joel Osment, a kid sees dead people and talks with them. He doesn't actively call them up, like a necromancer does, but he interacts with them and helps them out.

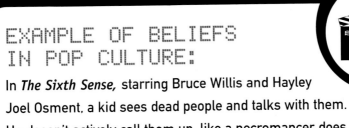

★ ★ CELEBRITY: ★ ★

Oprah Winfrey, talk show host. When Oprah was working on her movie *Beloved*, she claimed that she could hear the voices of slaves who were the subject of the movie. She said that she would even call them up to help her with her work.

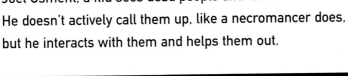

THE TRICK:

While there's a good chance that necromancy really works, the Bible makes it clear that it's wrong and we shouldn't get involved. Why? 'Cause the focus is on dead people, not on God and the amazing life He gives.

SCENE 1

Ouija Board
MAKING CONTACT

//occult religions and practices: section 3//

SHORT HISTORY

Ouija boards have been around in some form for a long time. People have been trying to communicate with dead people forever. During the nineteenth century, séances were prominent in Europe. People would sit around a table and wait for someone from the dead to speak to them. When someone from the dead wanted to speak, they'd tip the table or bang one of the table legs on the floor. When a table moved, or a table leg hit the floor, the medium (the person who led the séance) had the **ability to interpret** the signals and signs.

However, people didn't find this too exciting. In fact, many got bored at séances. So, mediums tried to make it more **interesting**. They'd supposedly go into a trance and speak to the dead. Some created elaborate mini shows that were all fake schemes to convince people that they could speak to their dead relatives. One of the gimmicks that mediums came up with was a board that had lots of letters and a sliding piece sitting on top of it. **This was the beginning of the Ouija board, although it underwent several refinements in the years following.**

In 1892, a businessman named William Fuld developed the final form of the board and began mass-producing it. Fuld made a fortune off of the Ouija board. He died in 1927 when he fell from a factory roof. Some people think his death was an accident, others think he committed suicide. Soon after his death, the family sold all legal rights for the board to the **Parker Brothers** game company. They've produced the boards ever since. You can walk into just about any toy store today and buy a Ouija board.

BASIC BELIEFS

The basic beliefs surrounding the use of Ouija boards are simple. You either believe that you can talk to spirits who are dead or you don't. There are two different beliefs about what happens when you put your fingers on the board and begin to ask questions.

• UNCONSCIOUS: These people believe that when you ask the board a question, the answer comes because you're unconsciously moving the thing without knowing it. They don't believe that there are any spirits involved.

• SPIRITUALIST: These people believe that the messages and answers coming from the board are of another world.

FOLLOWERS ARE CALLED:
Ouija board users

HOW DOES A OUIJA BOARD USER BECOME A OUIJA BOARD USER?

You buy the board, you open the box, and you follow the directions. **Using the board is simple too.** You place it on a table or on your lap, and then get a friend to help you. You put your fingers on one side of the planchette (the thing that you put your hands on and moves around), and your friend puts their fingers on the other side. Then, you ask a question and you allow the planchette to move to an answer. You may ask either a yes or no question, or ask a question that requires a simple answer that can be spelled out using the letters on the board.

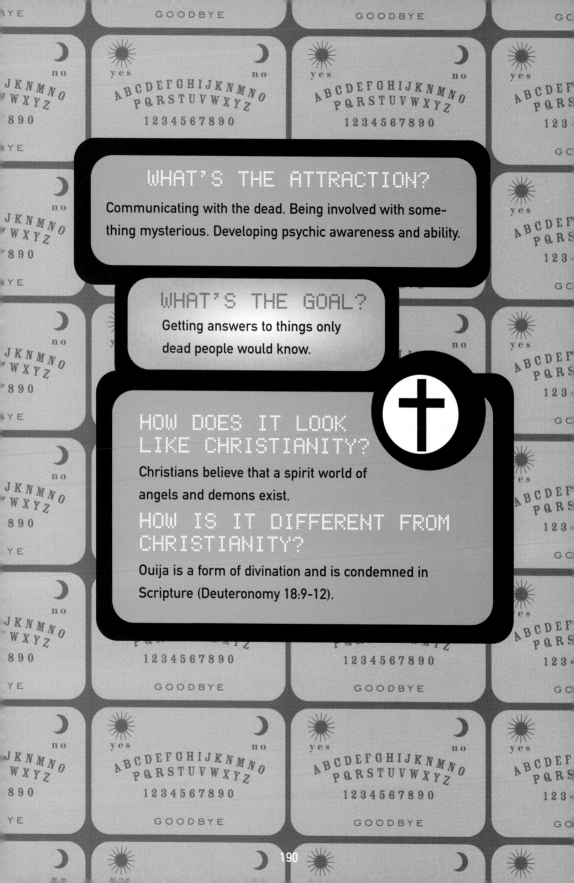

WHAT'S THE ATTRACTION?

Communicating with the dead. Being involved with something mysterious. Developing psychic awareness and ability.

WHAT'S THE GOAL?

Getting answers to things only dead people would know.

HOW DOES IT LOOK LIKE CHRISTIANITY?

Christians believe that a spirit world of angels and demons exist.

HOW IS IT DIFFERENT FROM CHRISTIANITY?

Ouija is a form of divination and is condemned in Scripture (Deuteronomy 18:9-12).

GOD:	There's no belief one way or the other about the god or gods who rule, run, or influence this world.
FIGUREHEAD:	None
AFTERLIFE:	It depends on the person, but by communicating with the dead, they demonstrate some sort of belief in an afterlife.
WORLDVIEW:	No position
SACRED TEXT:	None
WORSHIP SERVICES:	None
RITUALS / RITES / SACRAMENTS:	Jusing the Ouija board, usually at slumber parties and stuff like that.
DID YOU KNOW?	Ouija comes from the French and German words for "yes"—*oui* and *ja*.
GEOGRAPHIC CENTER:	None
NUMBER OF FOLLOWERS:	We don't know exactly, but Parker Brothers have sold millions of boards.

IMPORTANT VOCABULARY

PLANCHETTE: the thing you put your hands on to get the answers. When the Planchette moves, you get the answer to the question you asked.

EXAMPLES OF BELIEFS IN POP CULTURE:

SCENE 1

In the movie *Only You* with Marisa Tomei and Robert Downey, Jr., the plot is based on the main character using a ouija board to tell her the name of the guy she's going to marry. And in the movie *What Lies Beneath* Michelle Pfeiffer uses a ouija board to figure out what a ghost wants her to do.

★ CELEBRITY: ★

Morrissey has an album called *Ouija Board, Ouija Board*.

THE TRICK:

There's not a trick in the traditional sense—Christians believe that spirits exist. It's just that God tells us plainly that we shouldn't have anything to do with them. Read 1 Timothy 4:1 and Luke 16:26.

Parapsychology
READING MINDS

//occult religions and practices: section 3//

PARAPSYCHOLOGY

SHORT HISTORY

Parapsychology is a relatively new belief system. Actually, it's not *really* a belief system; it's more of an attempt to use science to justify a belief in the supernatural. It's probably best to break it down this way. On one side, you've got the paranormal—the belief that a dark or unexplained world exists beyond what our human senses can explain. Belief in the paranormal is an ancient belief, one that those who practice it have never had scientific proof to explain.

On the other side, you've got science. Now, science exists in a world of facts. Scientists seek to prove things through formulas or other things they can see, touch, or even (sometimes) just think up. Until the whole field of parapsychology arose, science and the paranormal were really far apart. But, in the mid 1960s, people from both sides came together and began asking, "Is there a scientific way to prove that the paranormal world really exists? Can we scientifically prove that invisible spiritual or mental powers do exist?"

Ever heard of ESP? (It's also known as Extra Sensory Perception, but we'll just stick with ESP). It's supposedly the ability to move objects with your mind, or even the ability to read other people's minds. ESP is where many parapsychologists began their marriage between science and the unseen powers of the human mind. In the mid 1960s, people began to ask, "Hey, I can read other people's minds, and I can even move things with my brain. Can I do some tests to prove what I can do?" Poof. Parapsychology was born.

Since parapsychology isn't a religious belief system, it's tough to pin these people down on what they think. **Parapsychology is more of a struggle to prove things than a system of beliefs.** But you can sum up what they think about the world through the following basic facts:

- Our minds have the power to do amazing things. We can move objects, read other people's minds, and use our mental powers to affect the physical world.

- Science can prove even unseen things. We can set up tests to prove the powers of our minds.

FOLLOWERS ARE CALLED:
Parapsychologists

HOW DOES A PARAPSYCHOLOGIST BECOME A PARAPSYCHOLOGIST?

Well, first you've got to believe that your mind can affect the physical world. Then, you've got to want to prove this assumption. Some parapscyhologists actually have advanced college degrees in psychology. There are many areas of study.

WHAT'S THE ATTRACTION?
Proving that you have super powers

WHAT'S THE GOAL?

Moving things with your mind. Reading other people's thoughts. Finding answers to questions about the supernatural.

HOW DOES IT LOOK LIKE CHRISTIANITY?

Parapsychology involves talking with forces beyond this world and using your mind to control things. Likewise, involvement in Christianity means communicating with God, who is not of this world. Christianity also involves using your mind for thinking, but not for controlling.

HOW IS IT DIFFERENT FROM CHRISTIANITY?

The goal of Christianity is to love God—not to have neat tricks you can impress your friends with.

GOD:	Depends on the person
FIGUREHEAD:	None
AFTERLIFE:	No position
WORLDVIEW:	Occultic
SACRED TEXT:	None

WORSHIP SERVICES:	None
RITUALS / RITES / SACRAMENTS:	**ACUPUNCTURE:** a Chinese practice of sticking needles into people in specific places to heal them
	ASTRAL PROJECTION: Not all parapsychologists practice this, but many believe in it. Astral projection is the process by which you project your spirit self out of your body and then you "float" around in this world—or in another plane of consciousness.
	DIVINATION: This is the process of trying to read different objects in a search for a hidden message.
	REGRESSION: A technique where someone remembers or is asked to remember an event earlier in their lives. It's usually used in hypnosis as a means to discover painful life experiences.
DID YOU KNOW?	Some parapsychology websites offer UFO abduction insurance.
GEOGRAPHIC CENTER:	Worldwide
NUMBER OF FOLLOWERS:	Unknown

IMPORTANT VOCABULARY:

EXTRASENSORY PERCEPTION: learning things supernaturally

TELEPATHY: paranormal awareness of another person's thoughts or feelings

PSYCHOMETRY: also called object reading, getting information about someone using one of his or her possessions or personal objects

PRECOGNITIONS AND PREMONITIONS: paranormal awareness of future events

OUT OF BODY EXPERIENCES: the process of leaving one's body and traveling to different places or times

AUTOMATIC WRITING: the ability to write messages without being in control of your body

PSYCHIC PHOTOGRAPHY: the process of taking pictures of dead people

THOUGHTOGRAPHY: the ability to produce images on film using your mind

MATERIALIZATION: the formation of a person during a séance

STIGMATA: marks on a person's body that resemble the marks on Christ's crucified body. St. Francis of Assisi is said to have had these marks.

SCENE 1

EXAMPLE OF BELIEFS IN POP CULTURE:

The classic example would be *Star Wars.* The jedi mind tricks and super powers that the characters develop for moving objects are exactly what parapsychology is all about.

CELEBRITY WHO BELIEVES: ★

The Amazing Kreskin (the world's foremost mentalist) has done telepathy and hypnosis on MTV, the *David Letterman Show*, and other programs. Howard Stern had him on his radio show and said, "I think he can really read minds."

A
Ace
A

THE TRICK:

Science, by definition, deals with the "natural" world, not the supernatural world. So you can't use science to prove these supernatural phenomenon.

Rosicrucianism
MYSTERY TO THE EXTREME

//occult religions and practices: section 3//

Think ancient Egypt. Why?

The Rosicrucian order goes back to about **1500** B.C. Back then, there were people who loved to study mysterious things. (Then, *mystery* meant "special knowledge" or "secret wisdom.") These people would get together and form study groups to learn about this stuff. Students had to demonstrate their desire to learn about these deeper kinds of things, and they'd have to pass a variety of tests. Over the years, people developed societies for which there were initiations. Meetings took place in nice temples, and there is speculation that they even met in the ancient pyramids of Giza (you know, those huge, old pyramids you always see on TV and in pictures).

Pharaoh Thutmose III is the guy who organized the first group. Many, many years later Greek dudes began to get in on this new school of thought. Philosophers named **Thales and Pythagoras** went to Egypt where they were initiated into the Rosicrucian beliefs. These guys brought the new ideas to the western world.

Okay, fast-forward through several centuries. In the late 700s A.D., the French philosopher Arnaud brought these teachings to France. It wasn't long before the Rosicrucian order had spread to most of Europe.

In 1694, a group of brave Rosicrucians hopped on board a boat headed to America. They braved the dangerous Atlantic Ocean led by the Grand Master of the Rosicrucian Lodge in Europe—Johannes Kelpius. They landed in Philadelphia and went to work. However, after they had been in America for awhile, people started losing interest and the order began to die out. Then, in 1915, a man named Dr. H. Spencer Lewis revived Rosicrucianism again in New York, and it has existed in the United States ever since.

BASIC BELIEFS

Rosicrucianism is full of secret meanings. The teachings and symbols express ideas that are evident on the surface, but they've got an altogether different meaning hidden underneath. Because they're so secret, trying to find out what they *specifically* teach is difficult.

What's the most important thing you've gotta know? These dudes are *borrowers*. If you read their history above, you already know that they've existed through all of the significant historical *and* spiritual traditions. As they existed in each of these times, they picked up various beliefs and practices and adopted them into their own beliefs.

Rosicrucianism teaches a philosophy of life, rather than a list of subjects or rules you've got to follow. They teach things that they say are totally applicable to your life. They believe that we all possess an inner energy that we never use to its fullest extent. They strive to teach us how to use our energy and power to understand ourselves and the universe, and ultimately that'll help us live better lives.

Let's say you wanted to become a Rosicrucian, or wanted to learn their philosophy. **What might you learn?** Here's a shopping list of things you can expect:

- your relation to the cosmos
- how to control your body
- the law of karma
- metaphysical healing
- how to contact the "Cosmic Mind"

Here's a few of the things they'd teach you if you decided to become an initiate into their order:

HUMAN DUALITY: People are dual beings—they have their five physical senses, and their psychic sense too.

THOUGHTS: Thoughts affect the physical world in different ways. You can enhance your ability to impact both the physical world and your own physical state through thought.

REINCARNATION: They believe that you come back to earth over and over until you've been good enough to "graduate."

FOLLOWERS ARE CALLED:
Rosicrucians

HOW DOES A ROSICRUCIAN BECOME A ROSICRUCIAN?

Well, they say you can stick with your current religion or church and leap right into Rosicrucianism without a hitch. Becoming a fully accepted Rosicrucian means going through various home study courses and some mentoring classes. It takes a long time of study and practice to become a full Rosicrucian member.

WHAT'S THE ATTRACTION?

Doing mysterious things. Connecting to a mysterious higher power.

WHAT'S THE GOAL?

Universal reformation. Through a change in thinking, a change in how you use your inner energy, you can help humanity attain a worldwide state of peace. This is a primary goal of the Rosicrucians.

HOW DOES IT LOOK LIKE CHRISTIANITY?

They are looking for an abundant life and how to get in touch with God.

HOW IS IT DIFFERENT FROM CHRISTIANITY?

They believe in reincarnation and karma.

GOD:	Depends on the person
FIGUREHEAD:	Benedict Spinoza, founder who lived in the early 1600s
AFTERLIFE:	Reincarnation
WORLDVIEW:	Occultic
SACRED TEXT:	The Kabala, a book of mysticism, believed to have come from the Jewish people
WORSHIP SERVICES:	Rosicrucians find validity in pagan worship, ancient Egyptian worship, Wicca, and other kinds of worship. So, (as you guessed) their worship services vary.
RITUALS / RITES / SACRAMENTS:	Rituals are highly significant in Rosicrucianism. Each time a person graduates from a level, their graduation is celebrated through a special ritual. The graduation rituals are different for each level.
DID YOU KNOW?	Rosicrucianism is believed to be the foundation for the Masonic Lodge. Many people believe that the Masonic Lodge is an evil secret society with strong occult practices.
GEOGRAPHIC CENTER:	Las Palmas, in the Canary Islands
NUMBER OF FOLLOWERS:	The actual number of followers is unknown. However, there are more than two hundred Rosicrucian lodges throughout the world.

IMPORTANT VOCABULARY:

MYSTICISM: the spiritual branch of science geared toward the attunement of the higher self. This is accomplished through meditation and contemplation.

METAPHYSICS: the plane that is outside the five senses—things like intuition, visualization, healing.

SCENE 1

The movie *The Skulls* comes close to this belief system—specifically their emphasis on brotherhood and fraternity.

CELEBRITIES:

★ Rene Descartes, philosopher ★ ★
Isaac Newton, scientist
Benjamin Franklin, founding father of USA

A
Ace
A

THE TRICK:

Rosicrucianism stresses the importance of improving the world through the spiritual upliftment of humankind. Trying to attain "spirituality" means finding our identity in and of ourselves. But this world is obviously full of sinful and evil people. The only way to find peace is to go to someone who isn't sinful. Who is, let's say, the Prince of Peace.

Shamanism

IF IT FEELS GOOD . . .

//occult religions and practices: section 3//

SHORT HISTORY

Shamans are masters of ecstasy. Not the drug, the feeling. This is what they're all about—getting a person to feel happy, detached, and free from pain. Shamans have existed in many different religions and beliefs. The Wiccans believe that Shamans can help you. Native American Indians trusted Shamans for years. Other religions have relied on Shamans for guidance, healing and information. So one thing to remember is that Shamanism is a practice that different people of different religions use.

BASIC BELIEFS

Shamans have particular specialties involving magic—like they can control fire or heal people. When they get someone into a trance, they believe their soul leaves their body and goes either into the upper world (the sky—to see the plan for their life) or the underworld (the earth—to see their ancestors) to look for ecstasy.

Shamans practice things like lucid dreaming where they can achieve an out of body experience. They typically communicate with spirits to achieve these states of ecstasy, but they keep control of their consciousness. Being possessed would be the exception rather than the rule.

This is connection with a spirit world. It can be dangerous stuff. On one Shamanic website there is a warning that certain types of trances and out-of-body experiences can cause death because the body can't sustain the vibrations from the spirit world. Kinda scary.

FOLLOWERS ARE CALLED:
Shamans

HOW DOES A SHAMAN BECOME A SHAMAN?

THERE ARE THREE OPTIONS:

1. You inherit the ability from your parents.
2. You get "called" to be one. Some people experience this when they have a near death experience and feel like they've been to another plane of consciousness.
3. You try to become one. You have to train with a Shaman to do this.

WHAT'S THE ATTRACTION?

Contacting other worlds

WHAT'S THE GOAL?

Helping others with their problems. Getting answers.

HOW DOES IT LOOK LIKE CHRISTIANITY?

They believe in a spirit world; Christians believe in angels and demons.

HOW IS IT DIFFERENT FROM CHRISTIANITY?

They attempt to contact these spirits to feel better. Christians know that God is our comfort and peace, and that He has the authority over the spirit world, not us.

GODS:	They believe that everything (literally everything) is divine.
FIGUREHEAD:	None
AFTERLIFE:	Shamans are often tied to a variety of belief systems. So, their belief in the afterlife or what it's like depends on the Shaman.
WORLDVIEW:	Animistic
SACRED TEXT:	None
WORSHIP SERVICES:	Don't have 'em. It's about personal experiences.
RITUALS / RITES / SACRAMENTS:	Shamans use different methods to achieve a trance state. Some of them are repeating sounds (like a drum beat), repeating movements, hypnotism, heat, sensory deprivation, drugs, posture, and dreaming.
DID YOU KNOW?	Shamans have a Spirit Spouse—this is a spirit that they believe they are having sex with and functions as their spouse. They also believe that they have animals in their family line.
GEOGRAPHIC CENTER:	Eurasia, Americas, and Australia
NUMBER OF FOLLOWERS:	12 million worldwide

IMPORTANT VOCABULARY:

GUARDIAN SPIRIT: a spirit that gives guidance and answers when out of normal consciousness

POWER ANIMAL: a spirit in the form of an animal that instructs

TOTEM: an animal spirit that is among your ancestors

ECSTASY: union with the divine

SCENE 1

EXAMPLE OF BELIEFS IN POP CULTURE:

The movie *Vanilla Sky,* starring Tom Cruise, Penelope Cruz, and Cameron Diaz, is all about Tom Cruise's character being in a Lucid Dream. It's like the lucid dreaming that shamans aim for—an out of body experience.

 ## CELEBRITIES:

Bob Marley, "reggae shaman" according to *Forbes* magazine

On the online game *Everquest* some famous shaman characters are Kumdan and Mudcrush

THE TRICK:

Shamans play in realms that we believe exist, but we also believe that they should be left to God to deal with. It's not safe to be calling up the spirits and asking them to take us to other planes of consciousness. If God wanted us there, He would have put us there. And since they have no organized beliefs, it's hard to know what they believe about eternity.

Satanism

EAT DRINK AND BE MERRY, FOR TOMORROW YOU DIE

//occult religions and practices: section 3//

 WARNING: The Church of Satan is a powerful and dangerous religion. As Christians, we believe that the devil is real and is a force of evil. He will be defeated in the last days, but for now he has limited power on earth. We recommend reading this chapter only after praying to be covered by the armor of God found in Ephesians 6 of the Bible.

SHORT HISTORY

You want the skinny on the Church of Satan? It's pretty simple. It was founded in San Francisco in 1966 by Anton LaVey, the star of the movie *Rosemary's Baby*, but the ideas really go way back in history. Since its founding, LaVey's philosophy and teachings have grown into other Satan worshipping churches and denominations. But most give their props to LaVey for his teaching and for helping them get their start.

The Church of Satan is legally recognized as a church; it is no longer considered a cult by the government.

Satanists try to make their religion all mysterious and secret. There's really no mystery to it. It's just the opposite of Christianity—do what Christians think is wrong. They worship the devil of Christianity. They believe the world is in a constant battle between dark and light, and they are fighting on the dark side. **All Christian sin is good, and all Christian good is evil.** Lots of Satanists also do the divination and black magic thing. They believe that in the end Satan will overthrow God and take over heaven.

They're all about materialism and hedonism. So when they say it's all about the spiritual world, that's a crock. It's about feeling good now—getting what you want to make yourself happy. Problem is, they aren't really all that happy. Satan is more of a symbol to them than a reality; **if he were a reality to them, they'd probably be scared to death.** What they're really about is worldly pleasure and sensuality. They want to get from the world all the pleasure they can, no holds barred. **They call on all kinds of evil spirits to get what they want.**

People who want to strictly adhere to the Satanic Church have to agree to the following nine statements.

• Indulgence

• Vital existence

• Undefiled wisdom

• Kindness only to those that deserve it

• Vengeance

• Responsibility only to those who are responsible

• The animal nature of man

• All "so-called sin" is the best friend the church has ever had

BELIEFS (CONT'D)

• **The Black Mass:** It happens on the witches' Sabbath. Most satanic groups practice it. The ritual reverses the Roman Catholic Mass, trashing the objects used in Christian worship. A lot of times a naked woman is stretched out on the altar where the high priest ends the ritual by having sex with her. Sometimes they drink the blood of an animal and eat human flesh in a mock communion. Human sacrifice—some still do it.

FOLLOWERS ARE CALLED:
Satanists

HOW DOES A SATANIST BECOME A SATANIST?

They believe that Satan exists; they attend a Church of Satan. They also believe the nine things under "Basic Beliefs."

WHAT'S THE ATTRACTION?

Getting to do whatever you want to make you feel good and not caring about anybody else. No rules except to enjoy yourself at all times.

HOW DOES IT LOOK LIKE CHRISTIANITY?

Well, it's just the opposite of Christianity. So they believe in the same important figures—God, Satan, Jesus, etc.—it's just that they've flipped it. Satan is the one they want to follow, and God is the one they want to defeat. But they would both agree that the world is in a constant battle between good and evil, Christians have just chosen the good side.

HOW IS IT DIFFERENT FROM CHRISTIANITY?

Well, again, it's the opposite. Christians don't believe Satan is good; they don't believe that he will win in the end. They do believe that he is powerful—which is why they are so serious about Satanism. They believe it is a real religion, and a dangerous one at that.

GOD:	Satan
FIGUREHEAD:	Anton LaVey, actor and author
	Michael Aquino, the high priest of The Temple of Set
AFTERLIFE:	Heaven—they think that Satan will conquer heaven. This is the exact opposite of what the Bible teaches.
WORLDVIEW:	Monotheistic, occultic
SACRED TEXT:	*The Satanic Bible*, by Anton LaVey. And they read other books about spells and rituals.
WORSHIP SERVICES:	In a temple
RITUALS / RITES / SACRAMENTS:	Some of these are really gross. Beware.
	• ANIMAL SACRIFICE
	• HUMAN SACRIFICE: murder or suicide
	• SEX CLUBS: any kind of sex or fetish you can think of
	• DRUGS: do whatever you want
	• DIVINATION: communicating with the demonic
	• CASTING SPELLS AND HEXES: to get what you want
DID YOU KNOW?	Notice in movies when the "devil" character is a beautiful woman—like Elizabeth Hurley in *Bedazzled*. He isn't always a slimy, fire-breathing creature.
GEOGRAPHIC CENTER:	United States
NUMBER OF FOLLOWERS:	20,000 in the USA

IMPORTANT VOCABULARY:

HEDONISM: the pursuit of pleasure above everything else

SCENE 1

EXAMPLE OF BELIEFS IN POP CULTURE:

Rosemary's Baby—Rosemary gets pregnant by the devil and has a horror child. Again, it's the opposite of Christianity.

 # CELEBRITIES:

Mick Jagger, legendary Rolling Stone, declined the role of Satan in a movie called *Lucifer Rising*.

Sammy Davis, Jr., performer

Jayne Mansfield, actor

THE TRICK:

Well, the trick here is that there isn't a trick. Satanism is real. All the stuff they believe in exists in a real way. But it's evil. Satanists hate God. They have "sold their soul to the devil." They are partners with the Father of Lies. Their whole lives are ruled by lies. It's no wonder that Satanism has always been associated with suicide, an indication that they're not having that great a time despite the fact that they are constantly seeking pleasure.

Tarot Cards

FORTUNE TELLING

SHORT HISTORY

Tarot cards first appeared in the 1400s in Europe. At the time, the church didn't allow people to read and write. See, the church had total control over people. If they kept them from reading and writing, then the pagan beliefs that many people practiced wouldn't spread. Instead of getting rid of their old spiritistic beliefs, common people were driven to hide their old beliefs and form clubs. People could pursue their beliefs or curiosities in these secret religious clubs. And they could do that without the church knowing what they were doing. Much of the teaching that floated around was said to be contained in tarot cards (but you've got to really look for them on the faces of the cards). And because most of the **teachings were done in private** and not documented, there isn't any recorded history about the early teachings contained in the tarot. As there is no historical record of what people were taught, we're left with almost nothing to read about the history of the time, or how the cards came to exist.

Since tarot cards aren't a religion, there's no **standard belief system attached to them.** People who use tarot cards differ in their beliefs about God, the afterlife, the spiritual world and those kinds of things.

Here's where it gets interesting. The level of dependence upon the power of tarot cards reflects your beliefs about the spiritual world. For example, if you believe that tarot cards can tell you the future, **then you might believe that tarot cards are used by God (or Satan) to communicate with us.** It's possible to use the tarot strictly for entertainment purposes. Lots of people who use them have no clue about their power.

Since tarot cards are used by a variety of people, it's possible for them to be used by people who believe all kinds of things.

FOLLOWERS ARE CALLED:

Tarot card readers

HOW DOES A TAROT CARD READER BECOME A TAROT CARD READER?

They study the art of it, just like with fortune telling or astrology.

WHAT'S THE ATTRACTION?

Knowing the future. Understanding more about yourself.

WHAT'S THE GOAL?

Deeper understanding of your life. Communicating with spirits.

HOW DOES IT LOOK LIKE CHRISTIANITY?

Some people think that God will use things like tarot cards to show us His plan for our future, but there's really nothing clearly similar.

HOW IS IT DIFFERENT FROM CHRISTIANITY?

Tarot is another form of divination that is condemned in Scripture.

GOD:	There's not really any god associated with tarot cards, although it is believed that demonic influence is definitely involved.
FIGUREHEAD:	None
AFTERLIFE:	Reincarnation
WORLDVIEW:	Occultic
SACRED TEXT:	Actually, tarot cards can be a text. Many people believe that tarot cards contain stories, and secret texts within the artwork on the cards. So, if you can look at them and get a story, great! Otherwise, there's nothing to read.
WORSHIP SERVICES:	None
RITUALS / RITES / SACRAMENTS:	None
DID YOU KNOW?	No one is an expert at using tarot cards the first time they use them. Actually, it takes years of practice to learn how to read tarot cards the "correct way."
GEOGRAPHIC CENTER:	Worldwide
NUMBER OF FOLLOWERS:	Tarot cards are used by many people in a variety of religions. It's safe to say that millions of people use them for all kinds of reasons.

IMPORTANT VOCABULARY

SPREAD: the way the cards are laid out during a reading. There are lots of different kinds of spreads.

ARCANUM: the word literally means "mystery." Each card is called an Arcanum.

MAJOR ARCANA: the twenty-two major cards

MINOR ARCANA: four different suits of cards. The Minor Arcana consists of the suit of Cups, the Suit of Wands, the Suit of Swords, and the Suit of Pentecles.

THE HIEROPHANT . THE LOVERS . THE CHARIOT . S
OF FORTUNE . JUSTICE . THE HANGED MAN . DEATH
VIL . THE TOWER . THE STAR . THE MOON . THE SUN
FOOL . THE MAGICIAN . THE HIGH PRIESTESS . TH
ROPHANT . THE LOVERS . THE CHARIOT . TRENGT
OF FOR . ATH
VIL . TH . SUN
D . TH . IESTI
THE HI . IOT . ST
OF FOR . DEATH
VIL . T . THE SUN
FOOL . ESS . TH
ROPHA . TRENGT
OF FOR . DEATH
VIL . TH . THE SUN
D . TH . PRIESTE
THE HIERO . T . ST

EXAMPLE OF BELIEFS IN POP CULTURE:

On a particular *Seinfeld* episode, George goes to have his tarot cards read and takes Elaine with him. The reader, who is pregnant, is smoking and Elaine gives her a hard time about it. So the reader quits her reading and refuses to tell George any more, just as she had begun to say something about his future vacation. George, of course, freaks out about the vacation, wondering what the cards had to say.

★ CELEBRITY: ★

Miss Cleo, tarot reader and psychic

THE TRICK:

Tarot cards are a means of communication with another world and, similar to fortune telling and Ouija boards, give us access to things we would otherwise not know. Tarot cards may not sound like a big deal to some—like something to just have fun with. But trusting in any form of divination places you in the hands of evil powers and the Bible clearly speaks against it.

VIL . THE TOWER . THE STAR . THE MOON . THE SUN
D . THE FOOL . THE MAGICIAN . THE HIGH PRIESTE
THE HIEROPHANT . THE LOVERS . THE CHARIOT . ST
OF FO TUN . THE HANGED MAN . DEATH
VIL . THE TOWER . THE STAR . THE MOON . THE SUN
FOOL . THE MAGICIAN . THE HIGH

Vodun
ZOMBIES AND VOODOO DOLLS

//occult religions and practices: section 3//

SHORT HISTORY

Vodun is an interesting mix of African beliefs and Haitian superstitions. Lots of experts think that Vodun started in Africa. They believe that it goes as far back as ten thousand years ago. It's really hard to prove that, though. Lots of people believe that it started during the slave trading years. Slaves were taken from Africa to many places—including Haiti. When they went to Haiti, the slaves took their belief system with them. There, it became more of a structured religion. Then, as people traveled between Haiti and Africa, they took the religion back to Africa. They also took it to the USA where, in New Orleans, Louisiana, it really began to grow.

During colonial times, people were killed for practicing Vodun. These days many people believe that Vodun is constantly changing and evolving. It has an assortment of beliefs and practices from other religions incorporated into it.

Vodun believes that everything has holy significance. Everything has a soul and spirit. That's called Animism. They believe that the bones of dead people have magical powers. The bones of noble people are especially powerful. They believe that one god exists. **They call this god Olorun.** There's a not-so-powerful god that comes with him named Obatala. Obatala's job is to create the earth and life.

They also believe in loads of other spirits who are collectively called the Loa. **Want to know who they are?**

• OGOU BALANJO: the spirit of healing

• BARON SAMEDI: the guardian of the grave

• YEMANJA: the spirit of the water

Voduns practice human and animal sacrifices. They have really torturous rituals that they perform. Heard of zombies? Well, you're smack inside the religion that says they exist. A zombie is the result of evil Vodun magic. It's the belief that after death someone can be brought back to life. They're totally under the control of the person that brought 'em back.

Ever seen a voodoo doll? They use those too, now and then. A voodoo doll is a doll that has been connected spiritually with someone you want to hurt. They make the connection, stick a pin in them, and cause all kinds of trouble.

FOLLOWERS ARE CALLED:
Voduns

HOW DOES A VODUN BECOME A VODUN?

Voduns go through an intense initial process. There are a whole lot of painful lessons (described as horrible torture) they have to complete.

WHAT'S THE ATTRACTION?

Controlling things. Connecting with the dead.

WHAT'S THE GOAL?

Worship of the Loa. Receiving wisdom from the Loa.

HOW DOES IT LOOK LIKE CHRISTIANITY?

People have compared the blood and flesh rituals of Vodun to Communion. Plus, Voduns worship "saints" like Catholics do.

HOW IS IT DIFFERENT FROM CHRISTIANITY?

They believe in talking to the dead. They think that bones are magical.

GODS:	Olorun. He's the chief god, but there are hundreds and hundreds of other ones that they worship.
FIGUREHEAD:	None
AFTERLIFE:	They believe that the dead can be brought back to life under the evil power of Voodoo—these people are called zombies.
WORLDVIEW:	Polytheistic
SACRED TEXT:	Sorry, this religion doesn't usually write things down. There's no text.

WORSHIP SERVICES:	In a building called a Hounfour. Each Hounfour has a Poteau-mitan (a pole) at the center. The god and the spirits communicate with people from this pole. There's also an altar in these buildings that has all kinds of symbols on it.
RITUALS / RITES / SACRAMENTS:	The Vodun religion has many rituals. They're all designed to get in touch with the dead. Each ritual contains some of the following:

- An animal is sacrificed. They're sacrificed to satisfy the hunger of the Loa.

- There's usually a meal of some kind.

- Drums get pounded on.

- There's a lot of dancing and chanting.

The Desounin ceremony is practiced when someone dies. After they are buried, the Desounin is performed. At this ceremony, the dead person's soul, their life force and the Loa (located in the head) are sent to the right places.

DID YOU KNOW?	Some people have compared Vodun to Catholicism because of the similarity between the Loa and Catholic saints.
GEOGRAPHIC CENTER:	Africa; New Orleans, Louisiana; Haiti
NUMBER OF FOLLOWERS:	50 million worldwide

IMPORTANT VOCABULARY:

LOA: a group of spirits and gods worthy of worship. These are contacted by a Vodun practitioner. Practitioners and Loa usually have a strong relationship with each other.

MET TET: literally means "master of the head." It's like a spirit guardian.

GHEDE: the Loa of the dead. He's a powerful healer and protects children.

YANVALOU: a Vodun dance. It means "supplication."

EXAMPLES OF BELIEFS IN POP CULTURE:

At some secular bookstores you can buy voodoo kits. Also, in the book *The Crucible*, there is a girl who plants a voodoo doll with a pin in the side of it so that when she fakes having a pain in her side another woman will be found out as a witch.

SCENE 1

★ CELEBRITY:

Lisa Bonet, Denise from *The Cosby Show*, plays a voodoo princess in the 1987 movie *Angel Heart*, but we have no proof that she actually believes the religion. ★

THE TRICK:

They worship a good god, but that god has no problem with them calling up zombies or hurting other people through voodoo dolls? Their god doesn't sound like he's that good after all.

Wicca
WITCHCRAFT AND WIZARDRY

//occult religions and practices: section 3//

SHORT HISTORY

Some people believe that Wicca is a direct religious descendant of the Celtic or Druidic religions. Others see it as a more modern creation—not even fifty years old. However, most believe Wicca, or The Craft, to be at least 25,000 years old. Starhawk, an expert on Wicca, believes the beginning of witchcraft was more like 35,000 years ago.

Some say that it was first a superstition associated with fire, animal fertility, and curing disease. As it developed into a religion, those who were involved in it recognized that a supreme deity existed, but they were unable to discover who or what it was. So, they created their own gods who were subordinate to the god they couldn't name. They slowly developed into the Druids, then into the Celts. From there, people slowly began to form the Wiccan belief system.

And still other people believe that Wicca doesn't have any roots in the Celtic/Druid earth-based religions at all. They believe that Wicca is a melting of Celtic and modern day philosophy.

Here's a list of people who have shaped the current history of the Wiccan religion:

CHARLES LELAND: wrote *Aradia: Gospel of the Witches* in 1899. The book deals with the goddess Diana.

MARGARET MURRAY: wrote *The Witch Cult in Western Europe* and *The God of the Witches*, which give historical accounts of the witch burnings in Europe.

GERALD GARDNER: wrote *Witchcraft Today* in 1954.

SILVER RAVENWOLF: wrote *Teen Witch: Wicca for a New Generation*

STARHAWK: wrote *Spiral Dance: A Rebirth of the Ancient Religion of the Goddess*

BUCKLAND: wrote *Witchcraft from the Inside* and *Buckland's Complete Book of Witchcraft*

BASIC BELIEFS

Wicca is an earth-based religion. It closely follows the lunar phases and seasons. Wiccans schedule their worship services and rituals according to the phases of the moon and according to the seasons that best celebrate nature and their connection to it. They are organized in groups called covens.

God, or the goddess, is in everything. All things must be treated with respect and as aspects of the divine.

WICCAN REDE: the basic code of conduct, "An ye harm none, do as ye will." Basically, as long as you don't harm yourself or anyone else you can do whatever you want.

RULE OF THREE: states that the energy from everything you do comes back to you three times as strong as you sent it out. If you cast a spell against someone, it'll come back to you with three times the power.

RESPECT NATURE: everything has a spirit. You've got to respect everything in the natural world and treat them like they're living people.

FOLLOWERS ARE CALLED:
Wiccans

HOW DOES A WICCAN BECOME A WICCAN?

The initiate must spend one year in apprenticeship before they can be fully accepted into the coven.

WHAT'S THE ATTRACTION?

Casting spells and controlling nature. Communicating with nature. Getting in touch with the grass between your toes. Owing no allegiance to anyone beyond yourself and nature.

WHAT'S THE GOAL?

Balance with all things.
Balance of self with nature.

HOW DOES IT LOOK LIKE CHRISTIANITY?

God exists. But, even though there is a belief in a god, the god that Wiccans worship is the creation itself.

HOW IS IT DIFFERENT FROM CHRISTIANITY?

The deity that is worshipped by the witch is both male and female. Christianity believes in a personal, knowable God. Wiccans believe in an impersonal deity that is a part of nature.

GODS:	The human mind is incapable of knowing what Christians call "God," and it's useless to even try and think about it. For Wiccans god is both feminine and masculine—so they believe in a god and a goddess.
FIGUREHEAD:	Raymond Buckland, Gerald Gardner, Stewart Farrar, Doreen Valiente, Silver Ravenwolf, Alex Sanders, and Margaret A. Murray, to name a few.
AFTERLIFE:	Another tricky aspect of the religion: some witches believe in reincarnation and something called Summerland. Summerland is a place you go after dying to wait for a new physical form. They don't believe in an actual heaven or hell.
WORLDVIEW:	Pantheistic
SACRED TEXT:	Witches often keep something called a *Book of Shadows*, which is their own personal spiritual diary that contains spells, spiritual thoughts, etc. Covens often keep one of these books for the whole coven.
WORSHIP SERVICES:	They often hold ceremonies in the woods at night. Why? There are a lot of reasons. First, because that's where the ancient Celtic tribes held their services (they worked all day, so their services often started at sunset). Likewise, modern Wiccans are busy during the day, and only have the night to worship. They also have their services in the woods because that's where they're closest to nature. They practice their rituals skyclad, naked, so they can be closer to nature.
RITUALS / RITES / SACRAMENTS:	MAGICK: This is seen as casting spells to affect positive change in society. They use all kinds of things to cast spells, including wands, knives, or crystals. Great care is taken to not cast a spell that will harm anyone. INVOCATIONS: There are a variety of these, and they are said to the elements (like earth, wind, fire), to the gods and goddesses, for strength, etc. These invocations are like spiritual poems.

RITUALS / RITES / SACRAMENTS (CONT'D):	**GREATER SABBATS (HOLIDAYS)**
	SAMHAIN: October 31st. Also known as Hallowmas.
	BELTANE: May Eve. Also known as Rudemas, Walpurgisnacht.
	IMBOLIC: February 2nd. Also known as Candlemas, Brigid, or Oimelc.
	LUGHNASSADH: July 31st. Also known as Lammas.
	LESSER SABBATS
	Equinoxes and solstices:
	WINTER SOLSTICE: December 19–22, known as Yule.
	SPRING EQUINOX: March 19–22, known as the Vernal Equinox.
	SUMMER SOLSTICE: June 21–23, known as Midsummer Eve, or Litha. The longest day of the year.
	FALL EQUINOX: September 19–22, known as Mabon. These days and nights are of equal length.
DID YOU KNOW?	Wicca is the fastest growing religion on college campuses in the US.
GEOGRAPHIC CENTER:	Europe and the United States
NUMBER OF FOLLOWERS:	200,000 in the USA

IMPORTANT VOCABULARY:

AMULET: an object that is magically filled that reflects negative energy

CHARE: infusing an object with your own power

DIVINATION: the art of discovering the unknown through a tool like tarot cards

EVOCATION: calling up the evil spirits

MAGIC CIRCLE: a circle made from personal power. Wiccans perform their rituals inside a magic circle.

IMPORTANT VOCABULARY:

PENTACLE: a five pointed star, represents the earth element

SAMHAIN: a Wiccan festival celebrated October 31st. It symbolizes the death of the Sun god and the coming of Pan, the male god, who represents the coming of death, which happens every year. This date is also known as The Day of the Dead.

FOUR ELEMENTS: earth, fire, water, and air

SABBATS: Wiccan holidays

EXAMPLES OF BELIEFS IN POP CULTURE:

The movie *The Craft* is all about witchcraft. *Sabrina, the Teenage Witch* is a TV show about a witch and her family. Also, the WB Network airs a lot of Wiccan shows like *Charmed* and *Buffy the Vampire Slayer*.

★ CELEBRITIES: ★

Cybil Shepherd, actor

Gloria Steinem, American journalist and feminist

THE TRICK:

The Wiccan belief system is a reflection of what is at the core of man's depravity—the desire to be as great or greater than God. By glorifying the creation rather than the Creator, Wiccans have put themselves in a position where they make all their own rules. God, though, by definition is the <u>one</u> supreme being. Everyone can't be god. It doesn't work that way. God is the best, the #1 being, so 20,000 people can't be that.

CULTS

Webster's Dictionary defines a cult as a religion that is seen as unorthodox or spurious. That means people think it's a perversion of the original. Most of the cults listed in this book are Christian cults—so they take the basic beliefs of Christianity and twist them into something "new" and different. The reason we put *new* in quotes back there is because most of these cults boast some new truth that they have learned since Jesus lived. That's what makes them unique. See if you can find these new truths as you read through the chapters. Cults also typically believe that you have to be a member of their group in order to receive salvation.

Christ • Boston Church of Christ • Dallas
Christ • Fort Myers-Naples Church of Chri
Cruc...
ist...Madi
urch...h of
eater...ke C
Christ...Church of Christ • San
nci...rist...urch
ist...I
iona...ern
risti...Dart
urch...rist
ntre...ch o
ist...ver
urch...hrist
tro...rque
urch...Chri
stor...of C
t M...s Cr
urch...hris
An...Chu
ist...Grea
o C...of
an D...isco
urch...st I
shir...nati
isti...al C

The Boston Church

MEGA-CONTROLLED MEMBERSHIP

//cults: section 4//

SHORT HISTORY

The story of the Boston Church starts with a guy named Kip McKean. He was a student at the University of Florida. While he was there he became friends with a campus minister named Chuck Lucas. Lucas led a campus movement that **focused on the concept of discipleship.** Basically, he felt that he, as a discipleship leader, should control the lives of students in his discipleship groups. Lucas, McKean, and others went out to more college campuses and planted satellite groups. Initially, the groups thrived, but before long people began to wonder about these weird discipleship tactics. McKean moved to Lexington, Massachusetts in 1979 and began a church there. The church was really strong right from the start; it went from thirty people to more than a thousand in just a few years. Some people made verbal attacks against the church, but, for the most part, their heavy-handed approach to discipleship and church control continued without complaint. The leadership of the Boston Church began to plant churches all around the U.S.

In 1988 the Tampa Church moved to break from the Boston Church movement for the following reasons: unscriptural control over members and churches, unscriptural leadership, and unscriptural exclusivity. After this and a few other disagreements, the church began to rethink some of its beliefs and practices.

NOTE: There are also Nasvhille churches, Chicago churches, Dallas churches, etc.

Like many protestant churches, the Boston Church is evangelical—its primary focus is reaching out to nonbelievers. But there are ways in which it differs greatly from Christianity. Here are a few of them:

SALVATION: You're not fully saved when you believe in Christ. To be saved, you've got to be baptized too. Where do they see this in Scripture? Check out Mark 16:16 for their belief + baptism = salvation formula.

BAPTISM: Generic baptism isn't true or effective. When you're baptized, you've got to be baptized as a disciple in the International Church of Christ by an ICOC minister.

FOLLOWERS ARE CALLED:
Christians

HOW DOES SOMEONE BECOME A MEMBER OF THE BOSTON CHURCH?
They go through their membership classes.

WHAT'S THE ATTRACTION?
The whole discipleship process. It provides one on one or personal training for Christian service, righteous living, and a strong personal relationship with Christ. You get a lot of attention here; you're not gonna feel left out, that's for sure!

WHAT'S THE GOAL?
Salvation, evangelism.

HOW DOES IT LOOK LIKE CHRISTIANITY?

They use the Bible and say they believe that it is absolutely true.

HOW IS IT DIFFERENT FROM CHRISTIANITY?

Christ alone is not enough for them, they've gotta have this intense discipleship method too.

GOD:	The God of the Bible
FIGUREHEAD:	Kip McKean
AFTERLIFE:	In heaven with God
WORLDVIEW:	Theistic
SACRED TEXT:	The Bible
WORSHIP SERVICES:	Typical services you might expect in a church. They tend to be charismatic.
RITUALS / RITES / SACRAMENTS:	Baptism, Communion
DID YOU KNOW?	For every three people who join, as many as two leave the church disillusioned. The ICOC has been banned from many university campuses.
GEOGRAPHIC CENTER:	Boston, Massachusetts
NUMBER OF FOLLOWERS:	100,000 worldwide

IMPORTANT VOCABULARY:

DISCIPLESHIP: the key to church organization. The head of the whole discipleship thing is the head of the entire church.

RECRUITING: Members of The Boston Church are strongly encouraged to seek out nonbelievers and invite them to attend their church.

LEGALISM: The Boston Church is considered legalistic in its approach to spirituality. Legalistic spirituality is spirituality that adheres more to the letter of the law in the Bible, but doesn't always try to keep the spirit of it.

EXAMPLE OF BELIEFS IN POP CULTURE:

SCENE 1

A dancer of the Alvin Ailey American Dance Theater says she "prayed not to get leading roles, but to lead someone to heaven," after becoming a disciple of the New York Church.

CELEBRITY:

David Thomas, aka "Speech," of the band Arrested Development

THE TRICK:

The individual must be baptized by ICOC ministers into the church. All other baptisms in other churches are ineffective. But the Bible says we're saved by grace through faith, not by an ICOC minister's baptism.

A
Ace
A

Children of God
FREE LOVE

//cults: section 4//

SHORT HISTORY

The family of **mega-love** started in the 1960s when "free love" was a huge deal. During the 60s, people were all about communal living (living together and depending on each other for everything). This was when the Children of God (also known as The Family) first started. The group was founded by a guy named David Berg—he had been an evangelist and youth leader. He is also known as Moses David. He organized coffeehouses that gave away free peanut butter sandwiches to get hippies away from the sex and drugs and free love lifestyle. Berg was married, but he got married again in 1969 (yep, two wives). He claimed to get revelations from God that made him an end-time prophet. Members of The Family believed that Moses David received direct knowledge from God as to how they should live. These revelations became known as "Mo Letters."

Early on, the group had several unique outreach ideas. One was called "Litnessing." Basically they tried to witness through literature. The other was called "Flirty Fishing." Female members were encouraged to go into bars and seduce unsaved men in order to get them saved. In 1977, David Berg introduced sexual sharing and encouraged open sex among members. Any kind of sex was cool except homosexuality.

Since then, the Children of God have settled down a bit. They still follow Berg's teachings, but they're not so committed to the whole sexual idea.

The group sticks fairly close to the basic beliefs of evangelical Christians except in the following areas:

- Everyone gets saved. They believe that eventually everyone will be saved and go to heaven.

- All Christian groups (like Baptists, Presbyterians, etc.) except The Family are not really Christians.

- Government is evil.

- Scripture is right and true, but in some cases the writings of David Berg are more important than Scripture.

- Sex is fun and should be enjoyed constantly. Sex should be the focus of your life.

- Jesus had sex with Mary and Martha.

- The Holy Spirit is a voluptuous woman, the Queen of Heaven, Queen of Love.

- God the Father is a "pimp."

- Jesus was conceived by the Angel Gabriel and Mary.

FOLLOWERS ARE CALLED:
Christians

HOW DOES SOMEONE BECOME PART OF THE CHILDREN OF GOD?
Join the church, live communally with a "family"

WHAT'S THE ATTRACTION?
Free love, belonging to a close family. You don't have to worry about loneliness 'cause you're always with friends. Beating "the system."

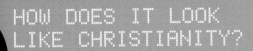

WHAT'S THE GOAL?
Evangelism.

HOW DOES IT LOOK LIKE CHRISTIANITY?

It claims to be Christian. They basically believe the Bible except for the things in the *Basic Beliefs* section.

HOW IS IT DIFFERENT FROM CHRISTIANITY?

Well, they believe that no one will go to hell. They think Jesus slept with Mary and Martha. They believe that the writings of David Berg can be more important than Scripture. Berg believed in continuing revelation. He distributed such "new" revelation through his "Mo Letters." Berg was also involved in astrology, the use of spirit guides and mediums. And he participated in necrophilia— sexual intercourse with spirits.

GOD:	The God of the Bible
FIGUREHEAD:	David Berg
AFTERLIFE:	Heaven
WORLDVIEW:	Monotheistic
SACRED TEXTS:	The Bible and the writings of David Berg. "Mo Letters"
WORSHIP SERVICES:	Traditional, in churches
RITUALS / RITES / SACRAMENTS:	When a new member joins the church, they're expected to give all of their possessions to the church. SEX RITUALS: Family members are encouraged to masturbate while they fantasize about having sex with Jesus.

IMPORTANT VOCABULARY:

COMMUNE: many people living in one place together sharing all their food, clothes, and supplies. People living in communes typically also share in the work of the house and other things.

FLIRTY FISHING (FFING): girls flirting with guys in bars so that they can sleep with them, then tell them about God

LITNESSING: witnessing to others through literature instead of the Bible

SHARING: basically fornication or adultery

SCENE 1

EXAMPLE OF BELIEFS IN POP CULTURE:

Okay, there's no famous movie about them or anything, but their ideas of living together and sleeping around are very common.

★ CELEBRITIES: ★

Rose McGowan, actor. Her father headed a Children of God group.

River and Joaquin Phoenix, actors. Their parents raised them in the cult.

THE TRICK:

The idea of trying to witness to someone by getting them to have sex with you makes no sense. The Bible says that sex outside of marriage is wrong. It's impossible to convince someone that they should live by the Bible when you're blatantly going against what the Bible says. And if they believe that everyone ends up getting saved anyway, why bother joining?

Christian Science
KEEPING THE DOCTOR AWAY

//cults: section 4//

SHORT HISTORY

Mary Baker Eddy (1821–1910). She's the lady who thought all this up, developed it, wrote the cult's most important books. Even though she's dead, she's still revered by Christian Scientists.

She was born into a strict religious home. Her parents raised her to be interested in the Bible. She was chronically sick, and that made her interested in healing. Mary had already tried everything she knew of to get better, so she began studying alternative ways. Her search led her to a local healer named Phineas Quimby. This guy was big into healing through natural methods and hypnotism. Through working with him, she started to get better. But one day she fell down and got seriously sick again. She kept getting worse, and when they finally realized that she was dying, she started to mentally prepare for death. But as she was reading some Scripture aloud about healing, she claims she was instantly healed.

After that Eddy hid from everyone and studied the Scriptures in an attempt to understand how it happened. When she thought she had figured it out, she wanted to share her newfound knowledge, so she wrote *Science and Health with Keys to the Scriptures.* It was a really controversial book—lots of people thought she plagiarized parts of it.

After the book was published, her beliefs became well known and were adopted in many places. Through the years, the membership of the Church of Christ Scientist has fluctuated. These days it's not growing significantly.

BASIC BELIEFS

This, like many other mind-based or consciousness-based religions doesn't have a strict creed of beliefs. **Here's some of what they think, though:**

- God is impersonal. All is God and God is all. God is Spirit-Mind.

- **They don't think that God is a Trinity.**

- Matter does not exist—it is illusion. Therefore, sin does not exist, and disease does not exist. Death does not exist, and evil does not exist. The solution to sin, sickness, disease and death is to realize they do not exist. They are illusions.

- **Man is spiritual and perfect. Man is incapable of sin, sickness, and death.**

- Christian Scientists draw a distinction between Jesus and Christ. Jesus was a man who lived in Palestine in the first century. Christ is the name of the true idea of God. Jesus is the human man, and Christ is the divine idea.

- **The virgin birth of Jesus happened spiritually, in Mary's mind. It was not a real physical event.**

- Salvation is of no concern since sin is an illusion and man does not exist (materially).

- **Man is incapable of sin.**

BELIEFS (CONT'D)

- The Lord's Supper is celebrated spiritually rather than with the physical elements of bread and wine (or juice).
- They think that belief in the Trinity is belief in polytheism.
- Jesus, as a man, was not divine. However, Christ is the name given to the true idea of God. So, Christ is not a person but merely a divine idea.
- They believe that *Science and Health* is equal to the Bible as divine revelation.
- The resurrection of Jesus was spiritual rather than bodily.

FOLLOWERS ARE CALLED:
Christian Scientists

HOW DOES A CHRISTIAN SCIENTISTS BECOME A CHRISTIAN SCIENTISTS?

By adopting their beliefs and practices, without going through any membership classes. Christian Scientists don't push church membership or evangelization.

WHAT'S THE ATTRACTION?

Christian Scientists believe that man is incapable of sin or evil. You get saved by believing that sin doesn't exist, it is an illusion.

WHAT'S THE GOAL?

To escape materially and embrace the Spirit—God

HOW DOES IT LOOK LIKE CHRISTIANITY?

They use the Bible in their worship services along with *Science and Health with Keys to the Scriptures.* However, when they use the Bible, they interpret it metaphysically.

HOW IS IT DIFFERENT FROM CHRISTIANITY?

They believe that man is incapable of sinning. Jesus was not divine; He was not God. *Science & Health* is equal to the Bible.

GOD:	God is Spirit. God is divine Mind, and Mind is all that exists. He is not personal, but is present in all things—including you and me. All that is not Mind (God) is material and does not exist, it is illusion.
FIGUREHEAD:	Mary Baker Eddy
AFTERLIFE:	Heaven and hell are not physical places. However, each can be an aspect of one's mental state. Ultimately, the individual is to become one with Mind (God).
WORLDVIEW:	Pantheistic
SACRED TEXTS:	The Bible *Science and Health with Keys to the Scriptures*
WORSHIP SERVICES:	Their worship services wouldn't be described as exciting or "contemporary." They don't have pastors. Church services are led by people called *readers*. These people read prepared lesson-sermons taken from both the Bible and *Science and Health* that are sent by The Mother Church.
RITUALS / RITES / SACRAMENTS:	They practice Communion without bread or wine. They observe Communion purely from a spiritual perspective. Otherwise, it would be material or physical and the material world is an illusion. Their goal is to acknowledge one's unity with God. They use the Lord's Prayer in their services.
DID YOU KNOW?	Weddings and funerals are not to be held in Christian Science churches. They are performed by ordained clergy from other churches. Lay people run Christian Science churches. They do not have professional clergy.
GEOGRAPHIC CENTER:	The Mother Church, Boston, Massachusetts
NUMBER OF FOLLOWERS:	400,000 worldwide 214,000 in the USA

IMPORTANT VOCABULARY:

PRACTITIONER: This is a person who comes in and prays for you when you're sick. They're used instead of doctors or surgeons.

MALICIOUS ANIMAL MAGNETISM: negative energy and negative mental power

MATTER: the opposite of Spirit; illusion, that which mortal mind (man) sees

EXAMPLE OF BELIEFS IN POP CULTURE:

You may be walking down a street in a big city, hanging out in a mall, or driving through a small town and notice a Christian Science Reading Room. These are places where anyone can come in and read the Bible and Mary Baker Eddy's book.

CELEBRITY:
Val Kilmer, actor

THE TRICK:

Ever heard of fatalism? That's where we say, "God's in control so it doesn't matter what I do." Well, He still gave us free will to make good and bad choices. Not going to the doctor when you need to is fatalistic. God provided healing resources for us to use for a reason.

Jehovah's Witnesses
WORKIN' FOR HEAVEN

//cults: section 4//

SHORT HISTORY

Have you ever had a couple of women or men, maybe with children, come to your door and want to tell you about God? Chances are they were Jehovah's Witnesses. From 1870-1875 a group of people in Alleghany, Pennsylvania, participated in a Bible study group that was later transformed into what is now known as Jehovah's Witnesses. The group was led by nineteen-year-old Charles Taze Russell (1852-1916), who became the founder of the church. The members of the group were known as "Bible Students," and within a short time there were two dozen Bible study groups. Russell wrote several books that helped the movement determine what their beliefs were. About thirty years later they started printing up little tracts to give to people, which were advertisements for what they believed. They used these tracts for their door-to-door witnessing. In the '90s, 1890s that is, the group started a magazine called the *Zion Watchtower*.

When Russell died in 1916, a guy named Joseph Rutherford gained control of the organization as the new president. He later, in 1931, changed the name of the organization from the founding name, The Watchtower and Bible Tract Society, to Jehovah's Witnesses. They were no longer known as "Bible Students."

According to the Witnesses, Jesus was to have returned in 1874. They also set several dates for the end of this world system. However, the dates of 1914, 1918, and 1925 proved to be wrong. These dates were when Jesus was supposed to return to take the "anointed class" (the 144,000 faithful) to heaven. Then again in 1968 the Witnesses predicted the end to come in 1975. When 1975 came and went, the Witnesses were disillusioned, and as a result, approximately 750,000 members left the organization by 1979.

BASIC BELIEFS

First, you've gotta understand that Jehovah's Witnesses think that the earth is here forever. Forever. It's where all the good people who aren't part of the anointed class going to heaven will end up. Here are some of their beliefs:

- God is called Jehovah.
- Christ is God's son, but he's not God. He's inferior to God.
- Christ died on a stake, not a cross.
- The earth will never be destroyed and will always have people living on it.
- The wicked people will be eternally destroyed.
- The human soul ceases to exist at death.
- Only 144,000 people will go to heaven.
- Observing the Sabbath as a rule ended with the Mosaic law.
- Man was created, then evolved.
- You must be baptized by immersion in a Jehovah's Witness church to be saved.
- The Holy Spirit is not God; He's an intelligent, impersonal force.
- The use of medicine and doctors is not allowed.

FOLLOWERS ARE CALLED:
Jehovah's Witnesses

HOW DOES A JEHOVAH'S WITNESS BECOME A JEHOVAH'S WITNESS?

Believe in God, get baptized as a Jehovah's Witness

WHAT'S THE ATTRACTION?

Gaining your salvation through your works.
Becoming a part of "God's Organization." Clear rules for living.

WHAT'S THE GOAL?

To be one of the 144,000
who will go to heaven

HOW DOES IT LOOK LIKE CHRISTIANITY?

Belief in God. They hold a high view of Scripture.
However, they restrict Bible reading without the aid
of the *Watchtower*.

HOW IS IT DIFFERENT FROM CHRISTIANITY?

They don't believe Jesus was God. They believe that only
a set number of people can be saved. Jesus said in the
Bible that He came for the salvation of all men, not just
144,000 of them.

GOD:	Jehovah
FIGUREHEAD:	They don't revere their founder like many other cults. Really, their figurehead would be the governing body of the cult.
AFTERLIFE:	Three options: HEAVEN: Only 144,000 people who are the anointed class will go there. You get to live with God. EARTH: This is going to be paradise, and it's for all the good people, the "other sheep," who weren't anointed. Those who were not Jehovah's Witnesses but attain perfection by practicing good things during the earthly millenium will receive salvation. NOTHING: This is for people who die. They just don't exist anymore.
WORLDVIEW:	Monotheistic
SACRED TEXT:	The Bible, New World Translation
WORSHIP SERVICES:	They hold their worship services in a place called a Kingdom Hall. They've got a lot going on in their halls throughout the week. Here are some of the things: PUBLIC TALK: This is where an elder gives a talk on a topic. Afterwards, they usually have a lesson based on the talk. MINISTRY PRACTICE: Once a week they show up and practice witnessing to people. They're also trained for specific ministry service.
RITUALS / RITES / SACRAMENTS:	Jehovah's Witnesses administer baptism by immersion only. The anointed class also receives the baptism of the Holy Spirit, indicating that they alone have become a part of the body of Christ. The anointed class celebrates the Lord's Supper once a year at Passover.
DID YOU KNOW?	They don't celebrate things like Christmas, Easter, Thanksgiving, birthdays, etc. They don't vote, salute the flag, or serve in the military, either. People who do these things get kicked out of the church.
GEOGRAPHIC CENTER:	Brooklyn, New York
NUMBER OF FOLLOWERS:	6 million worldwide 988,000 in the USA

IMPORTANT VOCABULARY

PUBLISHER: Jehovah's Witnesses that go door to door once a week telling people about their religion

DISFELLOWSHIPPED: the practice of shunning or excommunication, when a Jehovah's Witness violates a rule of the organization. Infractions could be things like talking to a former Witness or reading your Bible without the aid of the *Watchtower*.

SCENE 1

EXAMPLE OF BELIEFS IN POP CULTURE:

Blood Transfusions. Huh? Jehovah's Witnesses interpret certain Bible passages to mean they can't accept any form of blood transfusion. They believe life is a gift from God, represented by blood. Any person who receives a transfusion faces excommunication from the church.

CELEBRITIES:

Michael Jackson, pop legend, grew up as a Jehovah's Witness.

Ja Rule, rapper, also grew up in the cult.

Venus and Serena Williams, tennis stars, are actively involved.

THE TRICK:

It all sounds good. The Bible talks about the 144,000. It tells us to tell others about Jesus. The problem is, if only 144,000 people are allowed to spend forever with God, why did Jesus come? God's gift of eternal life is a gift, not something you've got to work for.

Mormonism
SECRETS AND WIVES

SHORT HISTORY

If you're going to study Mormonism, you've got to know this one all-important, unforgettable name: Joseph Smith. Smith was born in Vermont in 1805. During his teen years a revival broke out in his hometown. The revival was to eventually impact churches in several denominations, and as a result, **he was confused as to which church he should join.** Because he was concerned about what to do, he decided to ask God which church he should become affiliated with.

When he was fifteen Smith said that God the Father and Jesus Christ appeared to him and told him that all churches existing at that point were evil and he should stay away from them. Supposedly, this visit was followed by many more. After the first one where God showed up, the rest of the visits were from an angel named Moroni. On one visit, Moroni told Smith about a set of ancient gold plates that were buried near his home. After four years of appearances from the angel, Smith was finally allowed to dig them up, and he translated what became known as the *Book of Mormon*. He published his translation in 1830.

About the same time, Smith had organized the Church of Jesus Christ of Latter Day Saints and had several people following him, mostly family members. The church moved around a lot, but eventually settled in the small town of Nauvoo, Illinois. Because of their presence there, the town grew to be large. The local press published a story about Smith and the church's multiple marriage policies. Smith and his brother Hyrum, along with fourteen others, retaliated by rioting and destroying the newspaper office. As a result, Smith and the others were arrested and put in jail. After Smith was jailed a sympathizer smuggled a revolver to him for protection because the townspeople were agitated. They attempted a jailbreak, but were killed in the process. This event gave the fledgling church what it needed—a martyr.

After Smith's death, the church split into many other denominations and religions. Both Joseph Smith's nine-year-old son and a guy named Brigham Young (as in BYU, the Mormon university) felt they had the right to lead the church. Brigham Young eventually took control of the church, adding some of his own strange beliefs. He moved the group to Salt Lake City, Utah.

BASIC BELIEFS

When you listen to Mormons talk, their beliefs sound kind of normal. But, when you lay them next to what Christians believe, it's easy to see just how different their beliefs really are.

POLYTHEISM: Mormons believe that Jesus, God, and the Holy Spirit are three different gods. This is different from the Christian doctrine of the Trinity, which says that God is one being with three distinct revealed personalities.

THE HUMANNESS OF GOD: Mormons believe that God was once a physical person. They believe that right now, God has one or more wives in heaven.

THE HUMANNESS OF JESUS: Jesus was once a man who became God. He was only a physical man, not God the Son, while he was on the earth. Jesus was not the result of a spiritual act of the Holy Spirit in Mary's life. He was the result of Mary and Joseph having sex.

THE DIVINITY OF MAN: Mormons believe that each man, who is worthy, living on the earth will one day be the god of their own planet. They believe that each woman will one day live on the planet of which her husband is the god.

SPIRIT CHILDREN IN THE AFTERLIFE: A husband and wife will have the chance to have spirit children together after they're dead.

PRE-EXISTENCE: Mormons believe that before babies come to earth they exist in heaven. While they're in heaven they're learning things.

RACE: Mormons believe that African Americans are the descendants of Ham (Noah's son), and are black because their ancestors sinned and were cursed by God.

POLYGAMY: After governmental intervention, the church officially changed its position on polygamy and said that its members can't marry more than one person. However, there are still more than 25,000 polygamous marriages in Utah.

MISSIONS: Mormons who are really serious about their faith take a two-year mission trip, usually between high school and college.

FOLLOWERS ARE CALLED:
Mormons

HOW DOES A MORMON BECOME A MORMON?

First, you're invited to attend a series of six discussions that introduce you to the Latter Day Saints Church. After that, you can join by being baptized by immersion. Then they lay hands on you so you'll receive the Holy Spirit.

WHAT'S THE ATTRACTION?

The Mormons have a huge family emphasis. People are attracted to their strong family values and promotion of family unity.

WHAT'S THE GOAL?

Personal worthiness. Once you are deemed worthy, you can enter the temple and participate in the ceremonies for their dead and be sealed for all time and eternity with your spouse.

HOW DOES IT LOOK LIKE CHRISTIANITY?

A belief in God. Belief in heaven, though their understanding of both is not biblical.

HOW IS IT DIFFERENT FROM CHRISTIANITY?

They deny Jesus' essential deity. According to Mormonism, He is like all men—in that He became God through his obedience and personal worthiness. The whole idea that men get their own planets to rule after they die is not biblical at all. And Moroni the angel coming to Joseph Smith? Not part of the Bible either.

GODS:	The God of the Bible. But, remember—we're talking a totally different concept of God than Christianity believes. Also, men can become gods when they die.
FIGUREHEAD:	Joseph Smith
AFTERLIFE:	Only those who are proven worthy receive their own planet to inhabit. There are three degrees of heaven that one can obtain depending on their worthiness. There is no hell in the traditional sense however, there is spirit-prison hell that is a temporary state.
WORLDVIEW:	Polytheistic
SACRED TEXTS:	The Bible, The Book of Mormon, The Doctrine and Covenants, The Pearl of Great Price
WORSHIP SERVICES:	Worship services are held in either a branch or a ward. The temple is reserved only for the worthy Mormon who has received a temple recommend from his or her bishop. Mormon worship services are reverent and silent. Upon entering the church building, you won't hear much else besides whispering. There are no loud musical instruments.
RITUALS / RITES / SACRAMENTS:	**BAPTISM:** Mormons teach that baptism by immersion is a must for salvation. They do not accept infant baptism of any form. Once children reach the age of eight they are then baptized.
	BAPTISM FOR THE DEAD: Baptism is essential for a living person's salvation, but it is also needed to secure the salvation of those who never had an opportunity during life to believe Mormon teaching. Baptism for the dead is accomplished by an individual being baptized by proxy for one who has died, and must be done in the temple.
	THE LORD'S SUPPER: The sacrament is administered on a weekly basis for those who are worthy and who are eight years old and older.
	CELESTIAL MARRIAGE: Mormons are married for this life and eternity if they get married in the temple. Couples married in the temple also get spirit-children.

DID YOU KNOW?	Mormons do not consume any products that have caffeine in them—coffee, soda, chocolate, etc.
GEOGRAPHIC CENTER:	Salt Lake City, Utah
NUMBER OF FOLLOWERS:	11 million worldwide 6 million in the USA

IMPORTANT VOCABULARY:

UMIM AND THUMIM: Ever wonder how Joseph Smith translated the plates that the angel Moroni told him about? He had a sort of peep-stone, much like a crystal ball.

Smith put the seer stone, or peep-stone, in his hat and covered it with his face to read it.

SCENE 1

EXAMPLES OF BELIEFS IN POP CULTURE:

The movies *Your Friends and Neighbors* and *In the Company of Men* were both made by Mormon filmmaker Neil Labute.

CELEBRITIES:

Steve Young, NFL Quarterback

Roseanne Barr, actor, was raised as a Mormon.

Donnie and Marie Osmond, musical performers and talk show hosts

A
Ace
A

THE TRICK:

God has plainly said that His book (The Bible) is closed (you can check out His exact words in Revelation 22:18-19). Since most of what the Mormons believe is based heavily on their extra-biblical book that's full of all kinds of skeptical stuff, their beliefs really aren't founded on anything substantial. Plus, the Book of Mormon has no evidence supporting it, archeological or otherwise.

New Age
YOU AND YOUR AURA

//cults: section 4//

SHORT HISTORY

Okay, at this point—it's best to direct you outside this chapter. Why? Well if you'll go and look at the sections on Taoism, Buddhism, Christian Science, Parapsychology, Wicca, and Transcendental Meditation, you'll have a great understanding of part of the history of the **New Age movement** (and you'll grasp some of the foundational beliefs of these people too). The New Age movement is all about borrowing. They've just taken the beliefs of others and mixed them up—added their own stuff and made it a religion.

The New Age movement probably began as an idea thousands of years ago when people were **interested in mysterious spiritual kinds of things.** It lasted through the ages surviving in religions like Buddhism, Taoism, and then later in more western beliefs that studied non-Christian spiritual concepts. In the 1800s the movement was **fueled by Transcendentalist** writers like Henry David Thoreau and Walt Whitman.

These days it's a vital religion. Groups that track cults say that many Americans (even those who go to church) believe that some New Age ideas are true. Even though people believe these ideas, the New Age movement doesn't maintain one headquarters. It has not published a "bible." The concept of unity in diversity is left unadddressed.

Many New Age groups **have their own beliefs that other groups don't believe.** So, these basic beliefs are general.

- **GOD:** He's in everything—including you. He is in you, in the universe, and outside the universe. He's also an impersonal force that exists.

- **MANKIND:** not a sinful group of people. Rather, mankind is a group of people that are ignorant of their god potential. Humanity is divine and needs to realize it.

- **REINCARNATION:** Man evolves upward, not downward. In other words, you won't come back as a frog.

- **YOU AND YOUR AURA:** An aura is an invisible force or field that surrounds you. Some people say they can see it. Those who can see it say that it's multi-colored and shiny. People who read them believe they can tell how you're feeling based on your aura.

- **THE DEIFICATION OF MAN:** Man and God are one and the same. Man is evolving toward divinity. This process is known as God-realization. Man can eventually become a god.

- **THE PLANET (GAIA):** The planet is evolving the same as man is—it's getting better.

- **JESUS CHRIST:** Jesus was simply a man who became "the Christ." Christ represents the highest level of spiritual evolution for man.

- **SIN:** Man does not have a sin problem. Man's perception of sin is really a mistake. That which is thought to be sin is really ignorance. There is no need of salvation from sin.

FOLLOWERS ARE CALLED:
New Agers

HOW DOES A NEW AGER BECOME A NEW AGER?

Since the New Age movement doesn't have too much organization, you can't walk into a building and ask for a membership packet. The most common way to become a member or to be considered part of the New Age movement is to adopt the teachings and live them out.

WHAT'S THE ATTRACTION?

Spirituality that makes you feel good. Control your personal destiny. Peace and unity among all people regardless of race or religion.

WHAT'S THE GOAL?

To merge with the absolute "One" who is God. To realize your divinity.

HOW DOES IT LOOK LIKE CHRISTIANITY?

From the outside some things look the same, but when you get closer they aren't. Like that they believe in Jesus; yeah, but their view of Him is totally different than Christians'. Christians also believe that God is in their hearts—so in a sense, we share the belief that God is in us. But Christians don't think that they are God because of this, and they don't think God is in everything—only in His children.

HOW IS IT DIFFERENT FROM CHRISTIANITY

They believe that we are all God because God is inherently who we are. We have evolved through reincarnation. New Agers are as likely to follow the teachings of Buddha, Krishna, or any other mystic as well as Jesus. Jesus is not uniquely the God-man.

GOD:	Many different gods are associated with the New Age movement. New Agers do not exclusively follow any one teacher or teaching.
FIGUREHEAD:	None. They've existed for centuries without a leader.
AFTERLIFE:	Reincarnation
WORLDVIEW:	Transcendentalism-Pantheism, Monism and mysticism.
SACRED TEXT:	For them all religious texts are equally valid. However, they may have some difficulty with those that represent monotheistic (one god) religions such as Judaism, Christianity, and Islam.
WORSHIP SERVICES:	New Agers don't really have worship services. Some groups gather to celebrate or to study, but that's group dependent. There's no overall kind of worship service.
RITUALS / RITES / SACRAMENTS:	The New Age movement has lots of these. **ASTROLOGY:** the study of the stars to predict someone's personality or future. This has evolved in the New Age movement to include a religion based on the study of the stars. **CHANNELING:** This is where people can get themselves into a trance. While in their trance, they're able to invite the spirit of a dead person into their body. Some channelers are believed to be able to channel the consciousness of Jesus. **CRYSTALS:** New Age people believe that some rocks have the ability to heal or give power to those who wear them.

RITUALS / RITES / SACRAMENTS (CONT'D):	MEDITATING: Many religions practice this. In the New Age movement, the people have a different take on the meditative process—they seek to blank their minds out and see a higher consciousness.
	HARMONIC CONVERGENCE: This is when a bunch of New Age people get together at the same astrological time in different places and focus on world peace.
DID YOU KNOW?	Health food stores, yoga classes, and acupuncture clinics are all stomping grounds of many new agers—they have a strong focus on health.
GEOGRAPHIC CENTER:	The United States
NUMBER OF FOLLOWERS:	20 million in the USA

IMPORTANT VOCABULARY

ASCENDED MASTERS: these are people who have achieved the highest level of human consciousness. Their purpose is to help others get where they are.

COSMIC CHRIST: This is the belief that Jesus Christ is a force, not a person. The goal of this cosmic force is to guide people in spiritual evolution.

GNOSTICISM: This word has many ideas associated with it and goes back to before Jesus walked the earth. It's the belief that man's salvation comes through realizing his divinity.

GREAT INVOCATION: a famous New Age prayer that invokes the Cosmic Christ on earth.

MONISM: a metaphysical theory that views reality as a unified whole. God, you, your puppy, and your cheeseburger all come from the same stuff.

EXAMPLE OF BELIEFS IN POP CULTURE:

SCENE 1

In the movie *High Fidelity*, starring John Cusack, his ex-girlfriend moves in with a new age guru.

CELEBRITIES:

Shirley McLaine, actor

Deepak Chopra, author

John Denver, singer

Tina Turner, singer

THE TRICK:

Okay. They say that Jesus got the highest form of spiritual consciousness. But they don't believe that what He said is true—that He was God and He was the only way to be saved. So, is lying the highest form of spiritual consciousness?

Scientology
GETTING TO KNOW YOURSELF

//cults: section 4//

SHORT HISTORY

We're talking about a fairly simple history here. L. Ron Hubbard was a guy who wrote some really popular books, magazine articles, and movie scripts. He wrote about a lot of different topics because he traveled all over the world and saw all kinds of interesting things. You've heard of the "lowest common denominator" in math, right? Well, that's what he was looking for, but in people. Everywhere he went he tried to figure out what connected people—what about them was the same. Scientology at its best is a self-help religious system.

In 1938 he wrote a book called *Excalibur* that was never published. But while he was writing it, he got the idea for another book, *Dianetics* (it means "through the soul"), which he wrote in 1950. With this book his ideas gained popularity, and people started believing what he wrote. In 1951, he founded Scientology as a religious philosophy. The first Scientology church was formed in 1954 in Los Angeles. Scientology means "knowing how to know."

BASIC BELIEFS

Here's the scoop, according to L. Ron. You are a spiritual being. Basically good, not a sinner by nature. You have a mind and you have a body, but they are separate from the spiritual part of you. See?

The spirit. The way they see it in Scientology is that there is this spiritual life force, known as Thetan, that is in all living things. And the ultimate goal of all life for all beings is to survive for eternity.

There are eight ways (called "channels") you can do this: through your INDIVIDUALITY, your FAMILY, GROUPS, MANKIND, ALL LIVING THINGS, THE PHYSICAL UNIVERSE, SPIRITS, and GOD. Check how they get bigger as you go—from you up to the Universe. The best way to survive is to do the most good for as many of these dynamics, or relationships, as you can.

Okay. That was the spirit. Got it? Now let's look at the mind. The mind is the recorder. They believe that it keeps track of all the good and bad moments from this life and all your past lives. So, your mind is keeping track of all this stuff and, like a good mystery novel, you get clues (these "recordings") to figure out what's wrong with your spirit. Your mind also records painful moments in your unconscious mind (called "engrams")—problems you didn't know you had. These engrams or spiritual blockages that impede your spiritual growth can mess up your thinking at any time—kind of like a computer virus.

Auditors (people who listen) help you find and understand these traumas by using this thing called an E-meter. It's kind of like visiting a shrink. They believe you'll be a lot happier when you get rid of these engrams and live life without their side effects.

God exists but His identity is a matter of personal awareness and conviction. Jesus was one of many great teachers. You're on a search to understand yourself, others, life and God. Your job is also to help others and make the world a better place.

Scientology churches are places where people get together to study and receive counseling. Scientologists are actively involved in their communities through things like drug rehabilitation, park cleanups, revitalizing neighborhoods, fighting AIDS and more. Remember, their philosophy is that to survive for eternity you have to help out as much as you can.

HOW DOES A SCIENTOLOGIST BECOME A SCIENTOLOGIST?

You really don't have to join the group to become a Scientologist, but you can. You become one when you use their philosophy to understand yourself better, and apply those things to help yourself and others.

WHAT'S THE ATTRACTION?

The more you understand about yourself and life, the better you feel.

HOW DOES IT LOOK LIKE CHRISTIANITY?

They believe that Jesus existed. But they don't believe in Him the way Christians do. Jesus wasn't God, and the Bible isn't the only way to figure out who Jesus was. Members get to decide who they believe God is on their own, sort of make Him up as they go—that means that they don't believe in an unchanging Sovereign God like Christians do.

HOW IS IT DIFFERENT FROM CHRISTIANITY?

The whole focus is on this earthly life—not on God. You try to help people here on earth (which is a great thing), but the goal is for your survival for eternity. It's basically all about working to get somewhere, whereas Christianity is all about grace. Scientology teaches reincarnation as the outcome of life after death.

WHAT'S THE GOAL?

- A world without insanity, criminality, or war
- Helping others
- Understanding yourself
- Healing all your insecurities and hurts
- Personal harmony
- Higher state of spiritual existence
- To become an OT (Operating Thetan)
- To recognize your potential godhood

GODS:	Scientology offers a path to spiritual awareness and leaves it to the individual to come to his or her own awareness of God. That means the Christian God exists, but so do all the other gods people worship.
FIGUREHEAD:	L. Ron Hubbard
AFTERLIFE:	Scientologists believe that your spirit is immortal; it never dies. But when you die you don't go to heaven or hell. Instead, you are reincarnated on this earth over and over for forever.
WORLDVIEW:	Pantheistic
SACRED TEXTS:	L. Ron Hubbard's works: more than three thousand lectures, eighty-four films, and three encyclopedic series. His most famous book is *Dianetics*.
WORSHIP SERVICES:	Mainly they study L. Ron Hubbard's writings and lectures on Scientology and get personal counseling (auditing).
RITUALS / RITES / SACRAMENTS:	Scientology churches hold weddings, funerals, and naming ceremonies for its members, like you would find in most churches.
DID YOU KNOW?	Scientology's beliefs are most similar to Buddhism out of all other religions, but the methods of practice and application are new. Hubbard coined more than three thousand words to support his teachings.
GEOGRAPHIC CENTER:	The United States
NUMBER OF FOLLOWERS:	8 million worldwide 3 million in the USA

IMPORTANT VOCABULARY:

THETAN: your essence—god

ENGRAMS: blockages to spiritual growth

PRECLEAR: someone full of engrams

CLEAR: someone totally free of engrams

AUDITING: counseling to help look at your existence

E-METER: device auditor uses to discover engrams

OT: operating Thetan, you have arrived at your full potential

OVERT: one who questions the organization. They are shunned.

EXAMPLE OF BELIEFS IN POP CULTURE:

"A being causes his own feelings. / The greatest there is joy in life is creating. / Splurge on it!"
—rapper Doug E. Fresh, "The Joy of Creating"

CELEBRITIES WHO BELIEVE:

★ John Travolta, actor
Tom Cruise, actor
Jenna Elfman, actor

THE TRICK:

Scientologists believe that Jesus was one of many great teachers, but they don't believe that what He said was true. That doesn't make any sense—how can you think someone's a great teacher but think that what they said is stupid?

If there is no one true God, no creator in charge, then who decides if you've done enough good deeds? Who decides what your life will be like when you come back? And if you're here on earth forever, what's the point really?

Seventh Day Adventist
PREDICTING THE RETURN

//cults: section 4//

SHORT HISTORY

William Miller is probably the one person most responsible for the Seventh Day Adventist church today. He was a farmer in New York around the early 1800s. After exploring several belief systems, he eventually became a Baptist minister. Miller discovered that the Bible contained coded messages about the return of Christ. The more he studied, the more he discovered things like the specific date that Jesus would return, and when the end of the world would come. Miller decided that he couldn't keep all of this information to himself. So, he decided to begin preaching and writing about what he had discovered. BOOM. The beginnings of the Seventh Day Adventist church were formed, and the people within the movement were called Adventists.

Through more study, Miller discovered that Jesus would return on March 21, 1844. So, he wrote and preached about it to others, telling them to get ready, because Jesus was coming back on that date. When March 21 came and Jesus didn't return. Miller revised the date to October 22, 1844. Well, that day came and went too . . . no Jesus! People got upset with Miller and began leaving the movement.

After the group had **formally disbanded**, one woman named Ellen White gathered a small group of Adventists into a church. They called themselves the Seventh Day Adventists. White was able to attract some of the former Miller followers, and the church became a formal organization in 1860. They predicted the return of Christ several times, and **(like this is gonna be a big surprise)** they were never right. The current Seventh Day Adventist church doesn't do anymore predictions; they just believe Jesus is coming soon.

BASIC BELIEFS

The Seventh Day Adventist church mostly follows the beliefs of evangelical Christian churches. However, they do differ in a few areas.

- SOUL SLEEP: They believe that your soul is not immortal. So, when you die, you remain dead until Christ comes to wake you up.

- THE RETURN OF CHRIST: Jesus is coming back right now. That means you've got to be ready now. This belief has caused this group to make several incorrect predictions about the date of Jesus' return.

- BAPTISM: In order to be saved, you've got to be immersed. You can't be saved without this form of baptism.

- THE SABBATH: People who don't observe it aren't saved. If you don't honor the Sabbath, you'll be rejected by God.

- HEALTHY DIET: They believe that they should eat a healthy diet, avoiding the unclean foods mentioned in the Scriptures. They also don't smoke or do drugs.

FOLLOWERS ARE CALLED:
Seventh Day Adventists

HOW DOES A SEVENTH DAY ADVENTIST BECOME A SEVENTH DAY ADVENTIST?

The same way you become a member in any other church—you go through membership classes and join.

WHAT'S THE ATTRACTION?

Excitement about the return of Jesus

WHAT'S THE GOAL?

Evangelism. Worship.
Getting ready for the return of Christ.

HOW DOES IT LOOK LIKE CHRISTIANITY?

Belief in God. Trust in the Bible as God's Word.

HOW IS IT DIFFERENT FROM CHRISTIANITY?

Salvation is through baptism by immersion only.

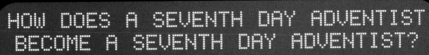

269

GOD:	The God of the Bible
FIGUREHEAD:	Ellen White
AFTERLIFE:	Heaven with God. But, only after Jesus returns. Until He returns to wake you up, you're stuck in your body . . . in your casket.
WORLDVIEW:	Monotheistic
SACRED TEXTS:	The Bible is seen as the authoritative Word of God. Also, many Seventh Day Adventist churches believe the writings of Ellen White to be true and authoritative.
WORSHIP SERVICES:	Just like any other church worship service: singing, Scripture reading, a sermon. They've got Sunday schools and vacation Bible schools.
RITUALS / RITES / SACRAMENTS:	The Seventh Day Adventist church has the same sacraments and rituals that most Christian churches have.
DID YOU KNOW?	Some people believe that the Seventh Day Adventist church *isn't* a cult. In recent years, many believe that the doctrine has been reorganized enough to make it just another Christian denomination with unique beliefs.
GEOGRAPHIC CENTER:	Washington, D.C.
NUMBER OF FOLLOWERS:	12 million worldwide 900,000 in the USA

IMPORTANT VOCABULARY:

The vocabulary for this church (beyond what's been pointed out in the above) would be the same as in any other churches.

SCENE 1

EXAMPLE OF BELIEFS IN POP CULTURE:

Because of their strict beliefs in a healthy diet according to Scripture, many Seventh Day Adventists are vegetarians. So, lots of vegetarian restaurants you see today are run by Seventh Day Adventists.

CELEBRITIES WHO BELIEVE:

Little Richard, singer
Take 6, gospel group

THE TRICK:

Jesus is coming back. But, the Bible makes it clear that no one can know the day or the hour that He will return. So, go ahead and predict all you want. Jesus is keeping it a secret. And the Bible makes it clear that we're saved by grace, not by baptism by immersion. Their focus is a little off here.

Theosophy
MIND OVER MATTER

SHORT HISTORY

Theosophy has two separate histories. The story begins with a cobbler named Jakob Boehme (1575-1624). One day the sun hit a pewter dish and reflected into his eyes. The reflection sent him into what he said was a vision of the godhead. He had many other visions and wrote them down in religious treatises. Boehme hung out with intelligent, quick-witted philosophers at the time, who challenged his way of thinking. His thoughts and ideas grew stronger as a result. Really, most of what he had to say was about "the godhead"— how the godhead could be limited and yet unlimited. He developed ideas about why the godhead had to reveal itself—why we know about it. Through Boehme's teaching, both written and spoken, a few people began to believe his ideas. Even though these few followers believed what he said, his philosophy never really caught on or spread to others. It wasn't anything too influential.

Many years later, a lady named Helena Blavatsky came along. She had studied the teachings of Boehme and began to build an entire society on what he and others like him had taught. Combining his teachings with early Greek philosophy, she formed the first, solid set of theosophical beliefs. Blavatsky traveled to India in 1878 to learn from Indian teachers. In 1895, she founded the Theosophic Society. Since then, theosophical ideas have spread and, these days, Theosophy claims to be more of a science than a mystical religion. Theosophic societies discuss religion combined with scientific ideas to form a unique blend of beliefs.

BASIC BELIEFS

   Okay, people, we're talking about some stuff here that you might not have ever heard of.

   Theosophy literally means "divine wisdom" (hint: it's from the Greek words *theos* meaning "God" and *sophia* meaning "wisdom"). Theosophy is best defined as a religious, scientific, and philosophic belief system.

   At its basic level, Theosophy says that there is one **unstoppable, undeniable source**. From that one source comes two distinct forms—spirit and matter. These two forms are connected and can't be separated. The two life forms (spirit and matter) are identical to the source. So, everything that comes out of the spirit-matter combination (which is everything) is part of the first source. Since that first source is divine, then everything is part of the divine.

   There are a lot of technical, scientific-type words and explanations that go along with this belief. Here are the basics.

- **INFINITUDE:** Everything is fundamentally one. That includes trees,animals, people, buildings, etc. Nature is infinite in time and space.

- **EVERYTHING IN THE UNIVERSE COMES FROM ONE SOURCE:** This source is boundless, eternal and completely unknowable.

- **WORLDS WITHIN WORLDS:** There are endless numbers of worlds within worlds.

- **SPACE AND TIME:** Space is infinite and is made up of smaller, finite pieces of space. Time is infinite and it is made up of smaller, finite pieces of time.

- **KARMA:** There is no such thing as chance. Everything is part of a whole and is infinitely connected. So when one thing moves, it will cause another thing to also move.

BELIEFS (CONT'D)

• **CONSCIOUSNESS**: Everything has a consciousness, including people, stars and planets.

• **THOUGHTS**: They're really tangible objects that exist on a higher plane. Every thought or action has an effect on our plane of consciousness and has a karmic consequence.

• **EVOLUTION**: All beings (that means everything) are constantly changing and getting better. All things are evolving. This includes people! They also believe in cyclic evolution—a being is born, lives its life and then dies. After death it waits to be replaced in another being or body. They call getting replaced in a body re-embodiment. Each new embodiment is the result of your karma (how you lived and all that stuff).

• **UNIVERSAL BROTHERHOOD**: All matter is related and connected. That means you're connected to stars, rocks, planets, and everything else you can think of.

FOLLOWERS ARE CALLED:
Theosophists

HOW DOES A THEOSOPHIST BECOME A THEOSOPHIST?
Well, you've got to buy into their ideas.

WHAT'S THE ATTRACTION?
Philosophy, thinking deeply about the universe. The whole pseudo-scientific connection.

WHAT'S THE GOAL?

1. to form a close brotherhood of humanity that doesn't exclude anyone

2. to encourage the study of all religions and beliefs

3. to investigate the unexplained laws of nature and the powers of divinity within man

HOW DOES IT LOOK LIKE CHRISTIANITY?

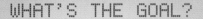

Both believe that everything in the universe comes from one source, but Christians believe that the one source is God.

HOW IS IT DIFFERENT FROM CHRISTIANITY?

They believe that Jesus as Christ is just a state of divine consciousness that we can all get—there wasn't anything special about Him. They are disgusted by the idea of His death on the cross—they think it was totally unnecessary. They believe in reincarnation.

GOD:	None
FIGUREHEAD:	Helena Blavatsky
AFTERLIFE:	You go through numerous cycles within this world. You get reincarnated until you no longer need the experiences found in this world.
WORLDVIEW:	Pantheistic, monistic
SACRED TEXT:	*The Secret Doctrine* by Helena Blavatsky
WORSHIP SERVICES:	None
RITUALS / RITES / SACRAMENTS:	In general, Theosophers are allowed to make up their own practices. However, many choose to do the following:
	MEDITATION: daily meditation
	VEGETARIAN DIET: Most theosophers avoid eating meat. They're also against wearing furs.
	RESPECT OTHERS: Theosophy stresses the necessity for each person to respect other humans, the environment, and animals. They're all about the idea of living out respect for everyone and everything.
DID YOU KNOW?	Lots of people think that theosophy isn't that different from Buddhism, and it's the basis for the New Age movement.
GEOGRAPHIC CENTER:	The United States, Europe, Australia, and South America
NUMBER OF FOLLOWERS:	37,000 worldwide 9,000 in the USA

IMPORTANT VOCABULARY:

MONAD: the immortal part of mankind that reincarnates into other beings, the spiritual soul

CASUAL BODY: the body you have right now, not your real body

GNOSIS: means "knowledge," studied by great philosophers who formed the groundwork of theosophy

ISWARA: the personal god, the divine spirit of man

MACROCOSM: the great universe

MAHATMAS: Spiritual Masters or Adepts who are evolved humans reincarnated. They, as Spiritual Masters, have given us the knowledge we need to evolve.

EXAMPLE OF BELIEFS IN POP CULTURE:

Some Theosophists say that *The Wizard of Oz* is an allegory of the way they view life.

★ CELEBRITIES WHO BELIEVE: ★

L. Frank Baum, author of *The Wizard of Oz*.

THE TRICK:

Theosophists say that, through reincarnation, we can continue improving, becoming closer to divine consciousness. It's a nice thought, but where is the evidence for this improvement? The laws of nature (specifically the Second Law of Thermodynamics) says that everything is moving toward chaos, not toward order. There's just no proof.

Transcendental Meditation
WE ARE ONE

//cults: section 4//

SHORT HISTORY

A guy named Maharishi, who lived in India, was a follower of another guy named Swami Brahmanand Saraswati Maharij, a well-known Indian guru. While under his teaching, Maharishi thought a lot about life and meditation. His teacher inspired him so much that Maharishi wanted to take what he had learned to America. So, in 1959, he went to the United States with his new style of meditation. It took off. Why? Because it offered a pseudo-religious way to inner peace and happiness that few people had discovered before. He gained a small following, including some celebrities. Eventually, however, people got bored. So, he went back to India to reorganize and rethink what he was doing.

A few years later, Maharishi returned to the U.S. He had removed the religious overtones and now promoted it as a scientific way to health and healing. Once again, it took off. People bought into the idea of meditation as a form of health and healing of the inner self. But after a few years, membership began to decrease, leaving the organization in kind of a mess. One of the reasons for the fallout this time was that scientists got involved and began studying the effects of Transcendental Meditation on people. They found that TM was actually bad for people, causing depression, mental tension, and anxiety among other things. In response to this, TM (at this point, an organized group of believers) developed studies to prove that it didn't hurt people, but was, in fact, actually helpful.

The same fight still goes on today. As things have progressed, people claim that the TM movement has swindled them out of their cash. There have been many lawsuits regarding this supposedly stolen money and the harm TM has caused people.

BASIC BELIEFS

TM borrows its beliefs from Hinduism. So, if you've read that chapter, some of those ideas will fit here. Here are some of the particulars of their beliefs.

- God is one impersonal being, but he takes on many forms. Many people believe that this is a form of pantheism—the belief that there are many equal gods.

- Humans are basically good.

- Each person has the impersonal god in them.

- Our problem is that we're disconnected from the divine being that lives in us.

- The art of meditation isn't just a mind clearing technique, it's a trek to get in touch with the inner god.

FOLLOWERS ARE CALLED:
Transcendental Meditators

HOW DOES A TRANSCENDENTAL MEDITATOR BECOME A TRANSCENDENTAL MEDITATOR?
By understanding, accepting, and embracing your inner-god's godliness

WHAT'S THE ATTRACTION?

Being at peace within yourself. Succeeding at your occupation through calmness and focus.

WHAT'S THE GOAL?

A state of consciousness called unity. Unity with the impersonal god, unity with yourself. Unity with others. Unity with your house. Unity with everything, but on an unseen consciousness level only.

HOW DOES IT LOOK LIKE CHRISTIANITY?

Their goal is unity with a god.

HOW IS IT DIFFERENT FROM CHRISTIANITY?

Their goal is also unity with everything. They believe in an impersonal god.

GOD:	One impersonal god who is known or seen in many different forms
FIGUREHEAD:	Maharishi Mahesh Yogi
AFTERLIFE:	Reincarnation
WORLDVIEW:	Monotheistic
SACRED TEXT:	Since they're closely connected with Hinduism, it's safe to say that they use the Vedas as their sacred texts. However, Maharishi has written some books that would be considered important to their beliefs. Here's a list of his books:

SACRED TEXT (CONT'D):	• *Science of Being and Art of Living* • *Maharishi's Absolute Theory of Defence* • *Maharishi's Absolute Theory of Government* • *Introduction to Maharishi Vedic University*
WORSHIP SERVICES:	In a temple
RITUALS / RITES / SACRAMENTS:	The whole process of Transcendental Meditation is a ritual. The biggest thing to remember in the whole TM ceremony is that the mind has to be completely relaxed. It can't exert any effort. In the process of meditation, the mind is supposed to dive into the universe and the Creative Intelligence (god). Their goal in the ritual is to get in contact with the great Creative Intelligence. When a person begins his or her walk into Transcendental Meditation, there is an initiation ceremony. A traditional Hindu Puja ceremony. The beginner brings flowers, fruit and a white handkerchief and puts it in front of a picture of Guru Dev. The teacher chants a song. The beginner then worships the Hindu Trimurti (the three main manifestations of Brahma). At the end of the ceremony, the beginner receives his or her Mantra. It's secret and supposedly created especially for that person.
DID YOU KNOW?	You can pay to take lessons in Transcendental Meditation.
GEOGRAPHIC CENTER:	worldwide
NUMBER OF FOLLOWERS:	3 million worldwide 1 million in the USA

IMPORTANT VOCABULARY:

YOGIC FLYING: This is something that happens during the meditation process. As you're meditating, your body hops forward several times. TMers claim that when this is done in larger groups, a ripple of love and peace is sent out into the world.

EXAMPLE OF BELIEFS IN POP CULTURE:

"Turn off your mind, relax and float down stream,
It is not dying, it is not dying

Lay down all thoughts, surrender to the void,
It is shining, it is shining.

Yet you may see the meaning of within
It is being, it is being"

—The Beatles, "Tomorrow Never Knows"

CELEBRITIES:

The Beatles, rock 'n roll legends, explored TM back in the '70s.

THE TRICK:

Okay, Transcendental Meditators believe in a group of gods. By definition "God" is <u>the</u> supreme, all-powerful being. How can there be more than one? There can't. They're searching inside themselves for gods that don't exist.

The Unification Church
PERFECT FAMILY FIRST

//cults: section 4//

SHORT HISTORY

The Unification church began with a guy named Young Myung Moon, currently known as Sun Myung Moon, who was born in 1920 to Presbyterian parents. When he began working in a friend's church, he realized that he had a divine appointment from God, but he didn't tell anyone. The more he worked, spirits told his friend that Moon needed to have the power of the church, and he should turn the power over to Moon. Eventually, his friend did that. After realizing that Moon was blessed to lead the church, Moon's friend began to get jealous of his power. The two of them split—Moon got the church. Moon began to teach his own ideas about God, and people bought it. His following grew.

About the same time, there was a woman in Korea with psychic powers named Mrs. Ho. She claimed to see and hear revelations from God. Her revelations became well known in her area of Korea, and people began to come to her for teaching. Soon, she had a following that developed into a church of more than one thousand people. She preached that God would be born again on the earth.

Moon heard about Mrs. Ho's teachings, which were similar to his. He was convinced that they should meet. They never actually did, but when she died, Moon inherited Mrs. Ho's followers. He combined them with his own to form the Unification Church (also known as the Moonies).

The Moonies have more than one thousand front organizations that help them get money and press time in the media, conservative organizations, and other mainstream groups.

- *The Divine Principle*, written by Moon, is equally as authoritative as the Old and New Testaments.

- Man is hopelessly corrupt both physically and spiritually. This corruption keeps man under Satan's dominion.

- SALVATION: Because Jesus died before he was able to marry, he was only able to redeem man spiritually. Rev. Moon, the Second Messiah, is going to redeem man physically and this physical redemption will bring about the kingdom of heaven on Earth.

- Jesus is not God in totality. He is only God in that He attained spiritual perfection. Jesus' divinity would have been total if He could have achieved physical perfection as well. Jesus' resurrection was spiritual and not physical.

- Moon is the Lord of the Second Advent, not Jesus. Jesus failed His mission. Moon is the Messiah, the one who returns and establishes the Kingdom of God on Earth, not Jesus.

FOLLOWERS ARE CALLED:
Moonies

HOW DOES A MOONIE BECOME A MOONIE?

They believe it and get involved.

WHAT'S THE ATTRACTION?

The church conveys a strong sense of family and acceptance. As a follower, you are a part of bringing the Kingdom of God to Earth.

WHAT'S THE GOAL?

- To unify all people of the world under their "true" parents—Moon and his wife
- To reach out to nonbelieving people and introduce them to the True Family
- To help end communism throughout the world

HOW DOES IT LOOK LIKE CHRISTIANITY?

Moon uses Christian terminology and events to develop his mysticism. Otherwise, the Unification Church is not at all like biblical Christianity.

HOW IS IT DIFFERENT FROM CHRISTIANITY?

They believe that Jesus failed in His mission to redeem humanity. Moonies accept *The Divine Principle* as scripture.

GOD:	The God of the Bible
FIGUREHEAD:	Rev. Sun Myung Moon
AFTERLIFE:	Hell is a spiritual domain for those who reject Moon as Messiah. It is ruled by Satan. However, the Lord of the Second Advent will ultimately redeem all of humanity and bring an end to hell. Once the redemption of humanity has been concluded, man will become a divine spirit and reside in heaven with God.
WORLDVIEW:	Monotheistic
SACRED TEXT:	They believe that the Bible has elements of truth in it, but is not truth itself. Rev. Sun Myung Moon's book, *The Divine Principle*, is considered truth.

WORSHIP SERVICES:	They have church in their worship centers on Sunday.
RITUALS / RITES / SACRAMENTS:	**FAMILY CENTERED:** Marriage and family are sacred. Members are supposed to strive to create the perfect family—one that will contribute to world peace.
	THE MASS WEDDING: You might have seen this one on television. Rev. Moon matches people up and marries them. Couples are allowed to back out if they want to. Just before the ceremony, couples participate in a Holy Wine Ceremony where they become free from their fallen nature.
	PLEDGE SERVICE: Celebrated on the first Sunday of each month and on January 1.
DID YOU KNOW?	Rev. Moon once performed a marriage ceremony for 6,516 couples at one time.
GEOGRAPHIC CENTER:	Japan
NUMBER OF FOLLOWERS:	1 million worldwide 30,000 in the USA

IMPORTANT VOCABULARY:

SECOND ADVENT: Moon believes that he's the lord of the second advent. The second advent is the second coming of Christ.

EXAMPLE OF BELIEFS IN POP CULTURE:

SCENE 1

"Yeah, big moon landing
People all standing up
Smiles for the loved ones
They go walking on down the aisles"

—James Taylor, "Line 'Em Up," referring
  to the Rev. Moon wedding ceremony with
  thousands of couples

CELEBRITIES:

Bill Cosby, actor and comedian, and Barbara Walters, journalist, were both recruited to speak at one of Rev. Moon's events, but when they found out he was behind it they backed out. Pat Boone, singer, and Jack Kemp, politician, stayed on after knowing Moon was involved.

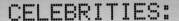

A
Ace
A

THE TRICK:

This is another religion where it's like, "what's the point?" Why would you do all of this work when Moon's gonna save you anyway? And then there's the fact that they believe in the God of the Bible, but they don't believe what He said is true. A lying God? Why bother?

Unitarian Universalist
MANY PATHS TO GOD

//cults: section 4//

SHORT HISTORY

During the beginning of Christianity, there was a group of people who loved God and religion, but who felt that there were many paths to get to God. These people thought that the one-way-through-Christ model didn't work, and they were intolerant of other beliefs. It wasn't until the mid-1500s that this school of thought became organized. In 1568 John Sigismund, a guy Unitarians call their king, helped issue the Edict of Toleration. This edict signified the beginning of the Unitarian movement. Soon after this edict, Unitarian churches were formed in Transylvania. Churches also began to spring up in Poland, but were persecuted and repressed. Unitarians faced persecution in other parts of the world as well.

The Unitarian movement eventually made its way to America with the Puritans. Many Puritans felt restricted by the tight rules of Calvinistic ideas and began to believe in the free will of mankind. Eventually, these people were the first Unitarians in America. The movement grew, becoming an established organization in Boston, Massachusetts in 1825, and has continued to spread all over the world since.

Unitarians are diverse in their beliefs. They believe that personal experience, conscience, and reason are the final authorities in religion. They're big on searching for truth in your own way and at your own speed. So, they don't really have a statement of faith or a creed or anything like that.

They also don't believe that the Bible is the only true Bible, or that the Christian Bible is complete. They feel that revelation is constantly unfolding and that the Bible is still expanding. So, new teachings and new prophets are just as valid as the ones in the Bible.

They believe that Christianity, Afro-American religions, Native American spirituality, and Wicca are all official, **valid sources of spirituality.** You've got a lot of options for whatever path you want to follow.

Their diverse beliefs can best be demonstrated by some of the following:

• Only one-fourth of them would say they're Christian. The rest could be Buddhist, Hindu, etc.

• Some don't believe that God exists.

• Everyone must seek their own spiritual path.

• Every religion has worth. No one religion is the right way.

• Every "bible" or other religious text has worth.

• You shouldn't have to stick to a creed or anything.

• Truth constantly changes.

• Everyone should be tolerant of others' beliefs.

• Jesus was a special person, but not the savior.

• You get saved by your works.

HOW DOES A UNITARIAN UNIVERSALIST BECOME A UNITARIAN UNIVERSALIST?

They join the church.

WHAT'S THE ATTRACTION?

Diversity of beliefs. Open to a lot of different views. They have little or no doctrine that a member must accept.

WHAT'S THE GOAL?

Harmony with humanity. Spiritual growth. Advancing causes like social justice, personal harmony, and peace.

HOW DOES IT LOOK LIKE CHRISTIANITY?

They believe parts of Christianity, like that Jesus lived and was a great person. But they don't believe that Jesus saved us or that He's the Son of God. They believe that the Bible is great, but it's not the only true Scripture.

HOW IS IT DIFFERENT FROM CHRISTIANITY?

Truth is not absolute; it changes. They don't believe that the Bible is the one true Scripture.

GODS:	All gods, possibility of belief in no god.
FIGUREHEAD:	William G. Sinkford
AFTERLIFE:	Very few Unitarian Universalists believe in an afterlife. They do not accept the possibility of hell. If there is any form of punishment it happens in this life. They say a loving God would not allow eternal damnation.
WORLDVIEW:	Atheistic, pantheistic
SACRED TEXTS:	Every spiritual text that has been written
WORSHIP SERVICES:	Church services are for human growth, with discussions of personal human issues, and of social or moral issues. God is almost never talked about. They also have sermons for kids, Sunday school, and other church-related activities.
RITUALS / RITES / SACRAMENTS:	FLOWER COMMUNION: Every year in late spring, Unitarian congregations celebrate the flower ceremony. Every member is encouraged to bring a flower and place it in a basket, symbolizing that they have brought something of themselves to the service. At the close of the service each person takes a flower, symbolizing that they have taken away something of someone else or something they've learned.
DID YOU KNOW?	Unitarian Universalists are fine with crossdressing and homosexuality.
GEOGRAPHIC CENTER:	Boston, Massachusetts
NUMBER OF FOLLOWERS:	600,000 worldwide 215,000 in the USA

IMPORTANT VOCABULARY:

BEACON PRESS: This is the Unitarian Universalist publishing house.

CIRCLE DINNER: This is a potluck they have for fellowship.

FREEDOM OF BELIEF: This is part of the Unitarian bylaws. Unitarians stress the freedom of each individual to pursue spirituality however they want.

STARR KING SCHOOL: This is the Unitarian Universalist seminary for training UU pastors.

WHOLENESS: Unitarians seek to reach out to nonwhite people and include them in their churches.

EXAMPLES OF BELIEFS IN POP CULTURE:

Unitarians actively endorse antigun legislation of any kind. Frank Lloyd Wright built a Unity Temple for the Unitarian Universalist Church.

CELEBRITIES:

Louisa May Alcott, author
Ralph Waldo Emerson, poet

THE TRICK:

Ultimately, you become confused because, if truth really is continually changing like they say, how is it truth? The very definition of truth is constancy.

Unity Movement
CAN'T WE ALL JUST GET ALONG

//cults: section 4//

SHORT HISTORY

The Unity Movement and Christian Science are the twin sisters of modern-day metaphysics. The essential philosophies of both were conceived by Phineas Parkhurst Quimby, a mental healer who discovered the power of mind over matter (the body).

The founders of Unity, Charles and Myrtle Fillmore, were briefly involved in Christian Science and got much of their spiritual philosophy from Quimby and Mary Baker Eddy.

In April of 1889 the Fillmores published their first magazine, *Modern Thought*. This was only the beginning of what was to become the largest mail-order religion in the country. The Fillmores adopted Unity as the name of their movement in 1895.

Charles and Myrtle had both developed an interest in the teachings of Eastern mysticism and incorporated ideas such as reincarnation, among others, into their philosophy. The Fillmores were extremely eclectic and borrowed ideas from a broad range of religious groups.

Unity stands for the unity of the soul with god, unity of all life, unity of all religions, and the unity of all men as they seek and ultimately find truth.

Unity opposes every doctrine of the Christian faith. They use Christian language with meta-physical interpretations, and to the unaware it appears to be Christian (biblical).

God is not personal. God is inherently within all humanity, whether they are Christian, Hindu, Buddhist, or atheist. Unity makes a distinction between the person Jesus and the Christ. Jesus is the man who embodied the Christ who is believed to be the spiritual or higher self, of every individual. Jesus shows us our divine nature. The Holy Spirit is the power of the Christ that lies within each of us, waiting to be awakened.

Scripture is not recognized as absolute truth. The Bible is only a part of divine revelation to man. Other sacred works are like-wise acceptable for living one's life. Sin is not real and has no power over mankind. Original sin is unreal and has no power as well. A belief in sin is simply wrong thinking. Sin, however, becomes real when man allows himself to give it thought. Death is an illusion and not real.

Man by his nature is divine. His true essence is that of being part of an impersonal God, manifested as a force. There is no need for salvation in the traditional sense, because sin is not real and therefore it has no power over man. Since man is God, he doesn't need to be saved.

FOLLOWERS ARE CALLED:
Christians

HOW DOES A CHRISTIAN BECOME A MEMEBER OF A UNITY CHURCH ?

The Unity Church doesn't feel like they should be your only church. They're totally comfortable with you being a member or a part of their church and a member of whatever other church you want. How do you join? They've got membership classes.

WHAT'S THE ATTRACTION?

Understanding your unconscious side. Using your mind to help control your body.

WHAT'S THE GOAL?

The goal is to achieve perfect union with the mind of God.

HOW DOES IT LOOK LIKE CHRISTIANITY?

A common worship setup. They use Christian language as an attempt to gain credibility.
They use Christian in their name.

HOW IS IT DIFFERENT FROM CHRISTIANITY?

The belief that man is not sinful, Jesus isn't God, and god is just a spiritual force.

GOD:	God is an impersonal deity. He is inherently within all humanity.
FIGUREHEAD:	**Charles and Myrtle Fillmore**
AFTERLIFE:	Heaven and hell aren't physical places you go to when you die. They're places you experience through your consciousness here on earth.
	Some Unity members believe in reincarnation. Others believe that our personalities die when we die, and we become spiritual beings.
WORLDVIEW:	Pantheistic
SACRED TEXTS:	Their official statement about the Bible is that it's a great book, but it's not the only great book to exist. Other books from other religions are worth studying and following too.
WORSHIP SERVICES:	A Unity worship service is like any other church service. They have singing, an offering, a sermon and meditation. They also don't limit worship to one day and one time. They believe that worship can and should happen anytime in the life of the believer.
RITUALS / RITES / SACRAMENTS:	Here's an interesting thing. Unity doesn't practice any rituals and sacraments. However, they do take a stand against traditional Christian rituals and sacraments. They reinterpret some of the following Christian rituals:
	BAPTISM: They don't believe that baptism is an actual sacrament that people should practice. They point out that Jesus never baptized anyone. Instead, they have something called Spiritual Baptism. This is a prayer experience with the Spirit. They call it the "ultimate dialogue between an individual and God."
	COMMUNION: The Unity church doesn't practice this ritual. They think it should be a private act between someone and God.
DID YOU KNOW?	The Unity movement has 1.3 million subscribers to their magazine, receives 2 million prayer requests every year, and sends over 30 million pieces of mail each year.
GEOGRAPHIC CENTER:	Unity Village, Missouri
NUMBER OF FOLLOWERS:	1 million worldwide 31,000 in the USA

IMPORTANT VOCABULARY

Consciousness: This is a huge word in the Unity Church. They believe that understanding and exercising our consciousness is a key element in the life of the believer.

EXAMPLE OF BELIEFS IN POP CULTURE:

Peace Incorporated and Y.O.U. Ralleys are both sponsored by the Unity Church.

★ CELEBRITY: ★

★ Wally Amos, founder of Famous Amos cookies ★

THE TRICK:

If Jesus Christ was the example of how we are to be our divine self, why did He say things that totally disagree with this philosophy? It just doesn't make sense that you'd pick a role model you think was a liar.

The Way International
WEAPONS, TROUBLE, AND WIFE SWAPPING

The Way

SHORT HISTORY

The Way International, founded by Victor Paul Wierwille (1916-1985), is believed by its followers to be the restoration of first century Christianity. Wierwille is said to have had an audible message from God that "He would teach me the Word as it had not been known since the first century if I would teach it to others."

Wierwille began teaching his newly discovered understanding of the Scriptures in his church and through his radio program. As the popularity of his abundant life message grew, he ultimately gave up his pastorate of the United Church of Christ in 1957.

He had developed his Power for Abundant Living (PFAL) course during this time, and it quickly became the cornerstone of his teaching ministry. It was through this course that Wierwille taught his unusual beliefs.

Wierwille was dynamic and proved to be a forceful speaker. He was convincing, yet manipulative. His primary target audience was young people, specifically those who were rebellious. The 1960s proved to be a great time for The Way to reach this kind of person.

Once Wierwille had officially incorporated The Way International in 1955, he established The Word over the World (WOW) Ambassadors. These WOW Ambassadors were essentially missionaries who spent one year of their lives establishing branches all over the world.

HISTORY (CONT'D)

In 1982 Wierwille named Craig Martindale, who had previously been involved in **Baptist Student Union** and **Fellowship of Christian Athletes** ministries, to head the organization. After Wierwille's death in 1985 and during Martindale's reign, The Way suffered a dramatic loss of 75-80% of its followers. Martindale had not only restructured the PFAL course and renamed it The Way of Abundance and Power (TWAP) course, he also demanded a strict obedience to himself as the new authority. As a result, the organization splintered into several (three at least) groups. These new groups remained faithful to Wierwille and PFAL.

BASIC BELIEFS

As stated earlier, Wierwille had some weird beliefs about Christianity. Perhaps the best known of all his writings is his book, *Jesus Christ Is Not God*. Wierwille, through PFAL, taught the following:

- God continues to reveal new understanding and interpretations of His Word—through Wierwille, of course.

- He taught that the four Gospels and the Old Testament were not to be used for Christian living, but they were only useful for education. He only accepted Paul's epistles as being useful for the body of believers.

- He not only denied the deity of Jesus, he also denied the Trinity, saying that it was of pagan origin. Jesus was sinless, but only human. He is our Savior and Redeemer, but He is not to be worshipped.

- He taught that Jesus' virgin birth was not a spiritual over-shadowing by the Holy Spirit, but a physical act between the Holy Spirit and Mary.

- The Holy Spirit is a synonym for God, not the third person of the Godhead. He differentiates between the Holy Spirit and "holy spirit." The latter is simply the power of God.

- Speaking in tongues is essential for salvation and right relationship with God. Tongues is a staple in their expression of worship.

- Baptism was a spiritual act and not one that involved water. He believed that physical, or water, baptism was a part of the law and that Christians were no longer subject to the law. It was a part of the old covenant.

- The most important day of the Christian calendar is Pentecost—the spiritual baptism of tongues.

- The Way differentiates between the body and the spirit. So if you get drunk or have premarital sex, those things don't affect your morality.

- They are deathly afraid of Satan and can only find comfort at Way meetings

FOLLOWERS ARE CALLED:
Wayers

HOW DOES A WAYER BECOME A WAYER?
They take the PFAL or TWAP course.

WHAT'S THE ATTRACTION?
Structured life, wealth, lots of young people in the movement

WHAT'S THE GOAL?

To recruit more members, speaking in tongues, a life of wealth and abundance

HOW DOES IT LOOK LIKE CHRISTIANITY?

They believe in the God of the Bible— their own version of Him, however.

HOW IS IT DIFFERENT FROM CHRISTIANITY?

For one, you have to speak in tongues to be saved. Christians believe that you are saved by grace.

GOD:	The God of the Bible
FIGUREHEAD:	Victor Paul Wierwille. After his death, Craig Martindale. Now Rosalie Rivenbark.
AFTERLIFE:	Commonly known as soul-sleep. There is no hell or eternal punishment. Although The Way has not written about the state of dead unbelievers, it can be assumed that they believe they would be annihilated.
WORLDVIEW:	Monotheistic
SACRED TEXT:	The Bible and Weirville's writings
WORSHIP SERVICES:	Their worship services are probably like yours. They play music. There's preaching. The only difference might be in the giving. The Way places a very heavy emphasis on tithing. They come just short of demanding that people give the ten percent God guides us to give in the Old Testament. They also require believers to give additionally to The Way organization.

RITUALS / RITES / SACRAMENTS:	The Way practices some of the sacraments that most Christian-type churches practice. You'll not find anything significantly new in their rituals and sacraments. However, The Way does not practice water baptism. They recognize a spiritual baptism that is centered on speaking in tongues as the evidence of one being baptized in the Holy Spirit.
DID YOU KNOW?	The Way members use techniques to speak in tongues that involve hyperventilation and are dangerous to your central nervous system.
GEOGRAPHIC CENTER:	New Knoxville, Ohio
NUMBER OF FOLLOWERS:	The Way does not encourage membership, but more than 150,000 people have taken their courses.

IMPORTANT VOCABULARY

The Way organizes their groups by calling them all parts of trees:

TRUNK: International Headquarters, Ohio

ROOTS: the Board of Directors

LIMB: the State Organization

BRANCHES: city-wide or regional ministries

TWIG: the local fellowship in home or campus

LEAF: each Way believer

EXAMPLE OF BELIEFS IN POP CULTURE:

If someone invites you to a Power For Abundant Living or The Way of Abundance and Power course, remember that that's The Way's initiation program!

★ CELEBRITY WHO BELIEVES:

We looked high and low but couldn't find a single one. Write us at www.xt4J.com if you know of one. ★

THE TRICK:

They believe in the Bible, but in their own interpretation of it. That means that they don't pay attention to the parts they don't like. For example, the part that says we're saved by grace, (not by speaking in tongues). You can't pick and choose parts of a book to be true. It's either all true, or none of it is.

GLOSSARY

95 THESES—the document Martin Luther nailed to the door of the church in Wittenberg, which condemned the Catholic church on 95 of its practices

AGNOSTICISM—the belief that man cannot know whether or not a god exists

ALLAH—the god of Islamic religion

ANIMISM—the belief in spirits outside of bodies, and that objects (like rocks or houses) can have spirits

APARTHEID—segregation, usually because of race

APOCRYPHA—books of the Bible that are in the Catholic Bible but not in the protestant and Jewish scriptures because of questions about authenticity

APOSTOLIC SUCCESSION—this is the way the pope passes authority to the next pope when he dies

ASCETICISM—strict self-denial, no pleasures

ATHEISM—the belief that no god exists

BAPTISM—a person is marked by water, either by sprinkling or immersion, as a member of the Christian community

BHAGAVAD-GITA, THE —a sacred text for Hindus and Hare Krishnas

BIBLE, THE—the sacred text for Christians

BISHOP—a leader in certain Christian denominations. They have the ability to ordain and confirm people (see ordination and confirmation) and they are in charge of a diocese.

BRAHMA—the god of Hindu religion

BURQUA—the material a woman living under Taliban rule must wear, covers all parts of the body

CHANTING—repeating Krishna's name in order to get closer to him

CHRISM—a mixture of olive oil and basalm used in Confirmation

COMMUNION—a Christian ritual where members eat bread and drink wine or juice to remember Christ's death and signify their spiritual union with Him

CONFIRMATION—a ritual where a Christian declares their belief in God and a leader asks that they receive the gift of the Holy Spirit, or in protestant churches they receive full church membership

COSMOLOGICAL—a part of metaphysics (abstract philosophy) that deals with the nature of the Universe

CULT—a religion that is considered to be unorthodox or a little deviant

DEACON—in the Catholic church he ranks right below a priest; in the protestant church he helps out with worship, pastoral care, and administrative duties; and in the Mormon church he is the lowest grade of priests

DEISM—belief in a natural religion that is based on morals, God's not personally involved with us

DHARMA—divine law for Hindus and Buddhists

DIOCESE—the administrative division of the church leadership in the Catholic church

ENLIGHTENMENT—a state of being where there is no desire or suffering

ENTROPY—the fact that the world is heading toward disorder rather than order

EURASIA—the area near the border between Europe and Asia

EXCOMMUNICATED—getting kicked out of the church

FAITH—being sure of God

FATALISM—the belief that everything that happens to us has already been decided, so it doesn't matter what we do, we can't change it

FENG SHUI—the concept that all your stuff goes in certain places in your house in order to get perfect balance

GANJA—marijuana

GNOSTICISM—the thought that all matter is evil, and we are free from that evil through our thoughts

GOD—the name for the God of Christian religion, a supernatural power

GURU—a person who has been liberated from suffering and desire in this life

HAIL MARY—a prayer to the Virgin Mary that asks her to pray for you. It goes, "Hail, Mary, full of grace, the Lord is with thee. Blessed art thou amongst women and blessed is the fruit of thy womb, Jesus. Holy Mary, mother of God, pray for us sinners, now and at the hour of our death. Amen."

HANUKKAH—an eight-day Jewish holiday that celebrates the rededication of the temple in Jerusalem

HINDU TRINITY—made up of Brahma, Vishnu, and Shiva

HOLY EUCHARIST—this is Communion in the Catholic church

HOLY ORDERS—what someone takes when they commit to give their life to the church, like being a priest or nun

HUMANISM—a way of life centered on human interests or values

HUMAN RIGHTS VIOLATIONS—imprisonment, torture or execution of innocent people

INDULGENCE MOVEMENT—in the 1400s, the Catholic church sold indulgences (forgiveness for past sins) to people to save their dead relatives from hell

IMMACULATE CONCEPTION—the idea that Jesus had to be born to someone who was perfect, so Mary was sinless

ISKCON—the International Society for Krishna Consciousness

KARMA—the idea that good works will be rewarded and bad works will be punished

KOAN—a riddle that forces you to give up logic and rely on intuition, a Buddhist thing

KORAN—the Islamic scriptures

KRISHNA—a god of Hare Krishna and Hinduism

MANTRA—a phrase you repeat (in Hinduism) to achieve a higher state of consciousness

MATRIMONY—getting married, in the Catholic church it's between two baptized members

MONASTERY—where monks live

MONISM—the belief that everything comes from one source

MONK—someone who has dedicated themselves to a life of solitude and poverty in order to serve God; don't get married, don't own anything, live in a monastery, etc.

MONOTHEISM—belief in one god only

NEW AMERICAN VERSION—the official Bible translation of the Roman Catholic Church

NIHILISM—the belief that traditional values are unfounded and our life has no meaning

NIRVANA—eternal enlightenment, no desire, no suffering

OCCULT / OCCULTIC—something that involves the supernatural in a secret way

ONTOLOGICAL—the argument that God exists based on the meaning of the word God

ORDINATION—to give someone official minister authority

PANTHEISM—worshipping all the gods of all different religions, God is equal with the forces of the universe

PARANORMAL—something you can't explain with science

PENANCE—doing something to show your sorrow over your sin, private confession of sins to a priest

PRIEST—in the Catholic church (and some others), a person in authority who ranks below the bishop but above the deacon

POLYTHEISM—the belief in many gods

POPE—the head of the Catholic church

REINCARNATION—the belief that when a person dies, his soul comes back to earth in a different body

RELIGION—serving or worshipping a god or supernatural being

SACRAMENT OF ANOINTING THE SICK, THE —asking for forgiveness and blessing for a person who's getting ready to die

SACRAMENTS—a Christian ritual that is believed to be a way to receive grace or a symbol of a spiritual truth

SACRIFICE—giving something you really love to God

SAINTS—in the Catholic church this is someone who is officially recognized as being especially holy; in the protestant church it is believed that all Christians can be called saints

SALVATION—rescue, by God, from eternal punishment for sins

SANCTIONS, POLITICAL AND ECONOMIC—a way to control another country who are breaking international law so that they'll quit breaking the law

SCRIPTURE—a collection of writings that are considered sacred

SECOND COMING OF CHRIST—the belief that Christ will return to Earth to claim His followers as found in the Bible

SECOND LAW OF THERMODYNAMICS—"The entropy of a closed system shall never decrease, and shall increase whenever possible." What does that mean? Well, entropy is the tendency to move toward chaos, so it means that, if left to our own, we won't move toward order and we'll tend to move toward chaos. It proves that evolution doesn't make any sense.

SEPTUAGINT—a Greek version of the Jewish scriptures

TAO—the way of the Universe, the way you should organize your life to be in harmony with the Universe

THEISM—belief that a god or gods exist

TORAH—the books that Moses wrote (the first five books of the Old Testament), the books of wisdom literature and the law that make up the Jewish scriptures

TRINITY, THE —God the Father, God the Son, and God the Holy Spirit are the three distinct personalities of the one God of the Christian faith

VEGETARIAN—a person who doesn't eat meat

YAHWEH—the God of Christian and Jewish religion

YIN AND YANG—the energy forces of good and bad that some believe control the world

YOGA—an ancient form of exercise and meditation practiced by many Hindus and Buddhists and other people

ZIONISTS—people who support the idea of a Jewish nation, Israel

GLOSSARY

INDEX

CHECK IT OUT!
GET INVOLVED!
MAKE A DIFFERENCE!

CHERNOBYL CHILDREN'S PROJECT

Help improve the quality of life of the kids affected by the Chernobyl radiation.
WWW.ADICCP.ORG

VOLUNTEER MATCH

Enter your zip code in this search engine, and it will tell you all the volunteer opportunities in your neighborhood.
WWW.VOLUNTEERMATCH.ORG

HABITAT FOR HUMANITY INTERNATIONAL

A Christian organization that welcomes volunteers from all faiths who are committed to Habitat's goal of eliminating poverty housing.
WWW.HABITAT.ORG

NATIONAL CENTER FOR FAMILY LITERACY

Promoting family literacy services across the United States.
WWW.FAMLIT.ORG

CHECK OUT THESE OTHER GROOVY PRODUCTS FROM EXTREME FOR JESUS™

BIBLES

The Extreme Teen Bible (NKJV)—HC	$24.99	0-7852-0081-9
The Extreme Teen Bible (NKJV)—PB	$19.99	0-7852-0082-7
The Extreme Teen Bible (NKJV)—Black	$39.99	0-7852-5555-9
The Extreme Teen Bible (NKJV)—Purple	$39.99	0-7852-5525-7
The Gospel of John	$1.50	0-7852-5537-0
Extreme Word Bible—PB	$19.99	0-7852-5732-2
Extreme Word Bible—Chromium HC	$29.99	0-7852-5733-0
Extreme Word Bible—Blue Snake HC	$29.99	0-7852-5796-9
Extreme Word Bible—USA	$29.99	0-7180-0153-2
The Extreme Teen Bible (NCV)—PB	$19.99	0-7852-5834-5
The Extreme Teen Bible (NCV)—HC	$24.99	0-7852-5835-3
The Extreme Teen Bible (NCV)—Retread	$39.99	0-7180-0063-3
The Extreme Teen Bible (NCV)—Reigncoat	$39.99	0-7180-0062-5

BOOKS

30 Days With Jesus	$7.99	0-7852-6626-5
Burn	$9.99	0-7852-6746-8
Daily Groove	$9.99	0-7180-0086-2
The Dictionary	$19.99	0-7852-4611-8
Extreme A-Z	$19.99	0-7852-4580-4
Extreme Answers to Extreme Questions	$12.99	0-7852-4594-4
Extreme Encounters	$9.99	0-7852-5657-1
Extreme Faith	$10.99	0-7852-6757-3
Extreme Find it Fast	$2.99	0-7852-4766-1
Extreme Journey	$14.99	0-7852-4595-2
Extreme for Jesus Promise Book	$13.99	0-8499-5606-4
Genuine	$13.99	0-8499-9545-0
God's Promises Rock	$3.99	0-8499-9507-8
Fuel	$12.99	0-7852-6748-4
Step Off	$19.99	0-7852-4604-5
Unfinished Work	$16.99	0-7852-6630-5
Xt4J Journal, Spiral-bound HC	$9.99	0-8499-9508-6